Frontrunners or Copycats?

Birgitte Tufte, Jeanette Rasmussen &
Lars Bech Christensen (editors)

Frontrunners or Copycats?

Copenhagen Business School Press

Frontrunners or Copycats?

© Copenhagen Business School Press
Printed in Denmark by Holbæk Amts Bogtrykkeri
Cover design by Morten Højmark
1. edition 2005

ISBN 87-630-0135-7

Distribution:

Scandinavia
DJØF/DBK, Mimersvej 4
DK-4600 Køge, Denmark
Phone: +45 3269 7788, fax: +45 3269 7789

North America
Copenhagen Business School Press
Books International Inc.
P.O. Box 605
Herndon, VA 20172-0605, USA
Phone: +1 703 661 1500, fax: +1 703 661 1501

Rest of the World
Marston Book Services, P.O. Box 269
Abingdon, Oxfordshire, OX14 4YN, UK
Phone: +44 (0) 1235 465500, fax: +44 (0) 1235 4656555
E-mail Direct Customers: direct.order@marston.co.uk
E-mail Booksellers: trade.order@marston.co.uk

Table of contents

Preface   7

Introduction: Frontrunners or Copycats?   8

1 **Understanding and Theorizing Modern Childhood in Denmark: Tendencies and Challenges**   20
JAN KAMPMANN
Children and the welfare state: From private to shared responsibility 20 / Children as political subjects 23 / The 'schoolification' of children 26 / Institutionalized individualization and individualized institutionalization 29 / New 'ideals of normality' 31 / The competent child as compulsive idea 32 / Persisting ambiguities in modern childhood 33 / References 35

2 **Children as Innovators and Opinion Leaders**   38
FLEMMING HANSEN AND MORTEN HALLUM HANSEN
Background 38 / The Theory of Diffusion of Innovations 39 / Social influence 45 / Innovators and opinion leaders 47 / Opinion leadership and innovators among children 50 / Overlap among innovators 53 / Overlap among opinion leadership 53 / From where do children get information about new products 54 / Conclusion and further research questions 56 / References 57

3 **Children, TV Advertising and the Law – Internal and External Perspectives**   60
LENA OLSEN
The problem 60 / The internal and external perspective of the law 62 / The applicable Swedish law concerning children and TV advertising 64 / An external view of the relevant legislation – the power of children to act 67 / Conclusions 75 / References 76

4 **Young People and Consumption: Commonalities and Differences in the Construction of Identities**   78
ANN PHOENIX
Consumption and young people's identities 79 / Reasons for buying particular things 82 / Consumption and transactions between children and parents 88 / Conclusion 95 / References 95

5 **Children and Promotion: The Role of Advertising and Marketing in Innovation** 99
BRIAN YOUNG

Advertising to children and innovation 99 / Changing media 102 / In summary …104 / Advertising in schools 105 / Dental health/diet/obesity 105 / What's on? 105 / Understanding intent 106 / Effects and influence 107 / Types of advertising 108 / Junk food! 109 / Celebrity endorsement 111 / Approaching the subject 112 / References 114

6 **Children and Adolescents' Use of the Internet – with Focus on Tweens** 118
BIRGITTE TUFTE AND JEANETTE RASMUSSEN

What is the Internet? 118 / International research 119 / Tweens 123 / What is the definition of 'tweens'? 123 / Tweens' Use of the Internet 125 / Concerns about the Internet 128 / Tweens – between media and consumption 129 / References 132

7 **The Invention of the Child Consumer: What is at Stake for Marketing Practice and Research?** 135
VALÉRIE-INÉS DE LA VILLE

Introduction: The child as a target for marketing management 135 / Part I – The progressive connection of children with consumption 136 / Part II – Children's consumerism: The new frontier of managerial practice? 144 / Conclusion: Toward a transformational agenda for marketing management and research 154 / References 155

8 **Children as Change Agents in the Pursuit of the Competencies of the Future** 159
ANNE FLEMMERT JENSEN

Prelude 159 / Background and purpose 160 / Why interest form a toy company? 162 / Results from LEGO Research among children 163 / Freedom, responsibility and performance 166 / Postlude 169 / References 170

Preface

Frontrunners or Copycats?

The idea behind the book 'Frontrunners or Copycats?' arose as a consequence of an international seminar on 'Children and Adolescents in relation to consumption and new media', organized by the Center for Marketing Communication at the Copenhagen Business School in September 2003.

The presentations of papers and the discussions during the seminar showed an enormous interest in the themes of the conference. From different disciplinary traditions, light was shed on whether children and young people in fact are innovators, to which extent, and in relation to which areas they are trendsetters, etc. The background for having the abovementioned seminar was that a great deal of focus has recently been put on children, consumption and media, although little research has been presented. Accordingly, a number of experts within the area were invited to the seminar, and most of the chapters of this book consist of rewritten and updated presentations from the seminar.

The book addresses itself to researchers, teachers, marketers, parents, students and others who want to keep abreast of the latest research within the abovementioned area.

We wish to thank all the authors for their contributions and interest in being part of this book. We would also like to thank Anette Nymark and Pernille Christiansen for their work with regard to reviewing the book.

Birgitte Tufte, Jeanette Rasmussen & Lars Bech Christensen
Copenhagen, 2005

Introduction

Frontrunners or Copycats?

BIRGITTE TUFTE AND
JEANETTE RASMUSSEN

The overall objective of this book is to give a broad variety of perspectives in relation to the important and on-going debate about children and adolescents as consumers. For this purpose, the articles cover historical perspectives on childhood, the concept of innovators, legal, generational and advertising perspectives and – not forgetting – facts about children's and adolescents' use of new media such as the Internet and their role as consumers in today's consumer society.

One could ask why it should be interesting and important today to focus on children and consumption. The answer is that there are several reasons, for instance the fact that children today are considered as consumers in their own right and at the same time exert an important influence on the family's consumption.

As expressed by McNeal:

'Young people can thus be recognized as a unique, all-important market in their own right'.

J.U. McNeal, 1992

Furthermore, according to McNeal, children and teenagers are:
- A primary market in their own right
- An influential market given their influence on parental household purchases
- A market for the future of all nations
- A particular demographic segment
- A specific life-style segment, according to the same criteria as their parents
- A benefit segment, such as educational benefits

Another reason for focussing on children and consumption is that with the globalization of mass media and brands, the patterns of consumerism among adults in general, and among children and adolescents in particular, are converging in most countries of the western world and, to a certain extent, the rest of the globe.

It is a well-known fact that children and adolescents spend considerable time on new media today. They have been quick to learn to use the Internet, and media and consumption are to an increasing degree intertwined today.

A third reason for discussing the theme is that we think it is extremely important to present the different concepts of children and childhood, which have been prevailing recently, and which are more or less behind different research approaches. Various surveys and studies have shown various results, often rigidly presented and perceived, as if the child is to be considered as competent or as vulnerable in relation to influence by media and consumption.

However, this dilemma is not a new one. Seen in retrospect, already in the 16th and 17th century, philosophers had different opinions. The English philosopher John Locke is of the opinion that the child has to be protected, and that it is the responsibility of the adult to guide and educate the child to become a rational and reasonable citizen. The French philosopher Jean-Jacques Rousseau considers the child as a kind of seed in a garden, where the seed has to grow and develop without too much interference from the adult.

However, during the past 50 years many voices have been emphasizing that the child ought to be considered as a competent and active person (Kinder, 1999; Kenway and Bullen, 2001/2003).

This means that within various disciplines, such as childhood studies, media studies and consumption studies, various definitions of childhood have been investigated and debated. As already mentioned, the paradigm discussed has been whether the modern child is to be considered as *a social becoming* i.e. a human being on its way to becoming an adult, or whether the child should be seen as a creature which is something in its own right i.e. *a social being.*

Childhood studies focussing on the abovementioned development, i.e. from a protective to a more equal attitude (between children and adults), have - on an international research level (Kline, 1993; Brembeck and Johansson, 1996; Kampmann, 2005) - to a wide extent been influenced by British sociologists (James, Jenkins and Prout, 1998).

In media research we have also had contradictory results and trends (Livingstone and Bovil, 2001; Livingstone et al. 2004; Tufte and Christensen, 2001; Buckingham, 2000; Kline et al., 2003), where various studies have ended up with different results, identifying the child as rather 'a vulnerable recipient' or a 'strong media user.

A parallel to this contradictory way of thinking is found in consumption studies in relation to children and adolescents (La Ville, 2005; Brembeck et al., 2005; Gunter and Furnham, 1998; Tufte, 2003).

To sum up, young people may be defined as innovators in relation to their insights and competences regarding consumption and media. Or they may – on the contrary – be defined as vulnerable creatures. As has already been said, some researchers and marketers consider the child as a social becoming, whereas others perceive the child as competent i.e. a social being. What emerges from such underlying assumptions – in relation to surveys and studies – are of course often, and as already said, opposite opinions. Furthermore, these different perspectives lead to different research approaches, practices and results, which have consequences for further academic studies and for the attitude and practice of practitioners when targeting children as a segment.

As will be shown, there is no general agreement among the researchers regarding to which extent children and young people may be considered as competent innovators/frontrunners or as human beings who need protection in relation to all the sources of influence they meet today. However, looking at recent research in progress (Rasmussen, Pynt and Tufte, 2004-2006), it seems as if they are often both innovators/frontrunners and vulnerable creatures in relation to new media and consumption. Children and young people are in a life phase of searching for identity, a time of peer orientation, because they often feel insecure. So a young person may on one hand wish to be considered as a unique individual, and on the other hand simultaneously wish to be accepted by the peer group. This apparent psychological ambivalence lies behind the title of this book.

The structure of the book

The common theme of the book starts with a rather sociological and psychological approach, involving the presentation of theories on how child and childhood have been perceived during different historical periods, and goes on to look at theories and reflections on children as innovators and opinion leaders as well as various foci on children and young people in relation to consumption and media – especially the

Internet and the role of advertising. Finally, the last chapters examine children from a more marketing-oriented point of view.

In the first chapter, 'Understanding and theorizing childhood in Denmark: tendencies and challenges', Jan Kampmann explores the concept of the competent child. He emphasizes that during the last 10-15 years extensive research has been done with focus on understanding and theorizing modern childhood. The research has focussed mainly on three perspectives: 1) how children seem to have changed, 2) how the conditions of modern childhood have undergone crucial ruptures and developments, and 3) that it is the understanding of and approach to children that have changed. It is the author's hope that his contribution will lead to further critical debates.

He presents how there has been a historical shift from children being in the family domain to a shared responsibility or a cooperative project between parents and the welfare state (which, among other things, provide child care). During the last 10-15 years, the political status and position of children in a broad societal context have also changed, and children are now seen as 'beings in their own right', 'as having agency' and 'of being competent'. This is closely connected to the Danish parliament's ratification of the UN Convention on the Rights of the Child in 1991, but equally so to an overall modernization of the Danish society. In continuation of this, the author talks about 'the schoolification of children' and 'institutional individualization and individualized institutionalization'. The former expression implies that, instead of teachers and parents explicitly defining rules and regulations, children are expected to act in accordance with cultural codes. The meaning of the latter is that when, for instance, conflicts arise among children, these are seen as problems in relation to which children are considered as individuals with individual rights, having the freedom to negotiate their own wishes and interests. Danish children are expected to attend and participate in public care facilities in order to be 'normally socialized' or socialized to be 'normal children'.

In chapter two, 'Children as Innovators and Opinion Leaders'[1], Flemming Hansen and Morten Hallum Hansen look at the role children can play in the diffusion of products. They use Everett E. Rogers' theory on 'Diffusion of Innovation' (1962, 1995) to illustrate that this theory also applies to children and that the picture of children as

---

[1] Published with written permission from *World Advertising Research Center,* Henley-on-Thames, Oxfordshire, United Kingdom.

innovators and opinion leaders is much in line with the general studies of diffusion of innovations.

Diffusion of Innovations is about acceptance of new practices, products and attitudes over time in a social system. The term 'acceptance' implies a decision-making process on behalf of the adopter in line with general decision-making processes in the study of consumer behaviour. The term 'over time' implies that the acceptance is increasing with time in a particular way, characterized as the diffusion process. In this diffusion process, the role of personal communication from opinion leaders, gatekeepers, change agents, sales people, innovators and others is important. Innovators are the first people to accept the innovation/product. Opinion leaders are persons from whom others take advice and whom they tend to copy in their behaviour. People are generally classified according to the time they adopt a new product or practice. The classification is the following:

- Innovators (2.5%)
- Early adopters (13.5%)
- Early majority (34%)
- Late majority (34%)
- Laggards (16%)

The findings presented in the chapter are based on a representative survey from 2003 covering 8-12 year-old children's media use, interest, activities and consumer behaviour. The overall conclusion is that the diffusion of innovation theory is relevant to use regarding children's adoption of products. Personal communication in the adoption process plays the most dominant role, meaning that it is the source children rely most upon, followed by television and advertising. Concerning the innovators, i.e. those who are the very first to adopt, they rely more on information sources outside the group (Internet, other media and advertising). The opinion leaders rely more on information from their social network (friends and school friends).

The third chapter, 'Children, TV advertising and the law – internal and external perspectives', is written by Lena Olsen from Sweden. The chapter focuses on the economic importance of children and emphasizes that in Sweden, despite the huge economic importance of children, the legislator has taken action only to a rather limited extent. The Swedish legislation relating to marketing is the Marketing Act, but there are no specific legal rules within this act that directly relate to children. It is thus, according to Lena Olsen, a fact that the legal problems which often arise in connection with children and advertising have not been given overall consideration by the legislator, even though there are a number of legal rules or other kinds of rules laid down by, for example, the Consumer Ombudsman of the International Chamber of Commerce (ICC) that deal with the particular difficulties concerning children.

The chapter falls into three parts. The first part deals with the internal and external approaches to law and the consequences of this from a methodological point of view. The second part deals with the Swedish legislation, using an internal perspective focussing on the substantial rules and describing the particular Swedish rules concerning children and advertising. According to this law, TV advertising that attracts the attention of children below the age of 12 is prohibited.

The third part discusses the field from an external perspective, the objective being to evaluate the power of the child in relation to children and TV advertising.

The chapter concludes by saying that the Swedish legislation has not realized that children are becoming still more important actors on the consumer side, and the author points at the fact that the Swedish ban only relates to children below the age of 12 years and furthermore is only applicable to advertising broadcast on a Swedish channel. Channels broadcasting from other European countries – even if broadcast in Sweden – are subject to the EC rules, which do not include a ban on TV advertising directed at children.

The chapter sums up by saying that the Swedish legislation in relation to advertising 'is apparently directed towards the child as a vulnerable social becoming'.

Chapter four, 'Young People and Consumption: Commonalities and Differences in the Construction of Identities', authored by Ann Phoenix, takes a closer look at the ways in which consumption is central to young people's identities and social relations. Based on the general literature and young people's accounts from three research studies, the author shows that there are some common themes in young people's constructions of consumption and in the ways in which social class, gender and race differentiate their consumption.

In the chapter, Ann Phoenix explores, among other things, the place that brands have in young people's identities. Brands are important for many young people's identity because they allow the construction of meanings, both actively and passively, and indicate the groups they want to identify with together with signalling status through style. Findings from the three studies show that there are differences in the importance of brands to identities; age, gender and financial (some cannot afford to buy brands) differences, and some deliberately choose styles that avoid brands.

She also looks closer at social class, ethnicity, gender and consumption. Her findings give an indication that a) social division in society is part of young people's consumption experiences and important to the ways in which they position themselves in their peer group, b) consumption is a symbolic process that is important to young people's identities and to divisions between them, and c) young people are aware of differences in consumption, based on choice of style group, social class, ethnicity, gender and age.

Concerning consumption and transactions between children and parents, she finds that consumption is a useful symbolic resource for allowing young people to demonstrate that they belong to their peer group and thereby allows the negotiation of inclusion. She also finds that consumption is important to identities, in that consumption produces insiders and outsiders in relation to the status that young people achieve through consumption.

The fifth chapter, 'Children and Promotion: The Role of Advertising and Marketing in Innovation', written by Brian Young, begins by presenting arguments for writing on advertising and marketing to children in a book on innovation by children and adolescents.

As is stated in other chapters of this book, the media landscape is changing in these years, and the author points to the fact that it is a media landscape in which promotion and marketing to children is rapidly changing and is virtually unrecognizable from that of 20 years or even 10 years ago. As part of this development, marketing strategies to children have also changed, and it is common practice for new brands to be launched on the back of other media representations.

It is further said that effects have a particular status in media research, where a stimulus (advertising) is presumed to have an effect at some level on a person.

In the article, various types of advertising are described, including advertising strategies for toys and for food.

In the second part of the chapter, Brian Young presents some cultural, anthropological and psychological approaches to children and advertising, and he emphasizes not only that there are a number of other theories than those based on development psychology, i.e. Piaget, but also that there is a need for further research in the area of economic socialization and consumer socialization.

The first part of chapter six, 'Children's and Adolescents' Use of the Internet – with Focus on Tweens', written by Birgitte Tufte and Jeanette Rasmussen, describes the rapid development of the Internet from being a tool developed for military purposes in the 1960's to being an everyday phenomenon in most people's daily life in the industrialized part of the world.

The second part of the chapter is concerned with tweens' use of the Internet.

First, the various concepts of 'tweens' are discussed. Researchers and marketers are using the term 'tweens as a group 'in between', i.e. between childhood and adolescents. However, some consider the group to cover children from 8-14, whereas others define the group as 8-12 year-olds – and some distinguish between younger and older tweens, i.e. 8-10 year-olds and 11-12 year-olds.

The chapter presents Danish qualitative and quantitative studies regarding tweens' use of the computer and the Internet.

Much concern regarding children's use of the media has been expressed by various parties, including parents, teachers and politicians, and the role and responsibility of the family has been on the agenda. However, families are different and have different attitudes to media and consumption, with the article distinguishing between four different types of families.

The chapter concludes by describing a two-year on-going research project 'Tweens between Media and Consumption'. The aim of the project is to examine to which extent the media play a role in consumer socialization for 10-12 year-olds in relation to other socialization factors such as family, school and friends.

Methodologically, the project uses quantitative as well as qualitative data, and hopefully the first results will be available in the autumn of 2005.

The next chapter, 'The Invention of the Child Consumer: what is at stake for marketing practice', is written by Valérie-Inés de La Ville.

The author begins with a discussion of the concept of the child as a target for marketing management, and emphasizes that it is very important not to reduce the child to a mere 'ego consumans' – with reference to Baudrillard.

The change in family patterns is discussed, pointing at the development from the former model of parent-child relationship to a more egalitarian way of relations between parents and children; a change which leads to consequences such as the recognition of children' agency, the recognition of children's cultures, and the importance of children's socialization.

An important aspect of looking at children as consumers is that children have their own money – pocket money, money received from grandparents, and money earned by themselves. This means that they have a purchasing power which is of great interest to marketers and advertisers.

According to La Ville, there has been a development in research regarding children as consumers, from looking at children from a rational decision-making approach to a more activity-oriented approach, and she proposes that child consumption should be regarded as a mediated social activity.

In the second part of the chapter, La Ville states that the field of children's consumerism can be perceived as a system of social practices which consist of five intertwined co-evolving sub-systems: 1) a relation system, which covers the relationship among the members of the family, teachers and peers; 2) an institutional system, which includes the different institutions that play a role in the life of the child; 3) a plurimedia system, which comprises all the media that a modern child uses; 4) a narrative system, which gathers stories etc. that the child knows and recognizes; and 5) an economic system, which includes, among other things, the children-oriented markets and the different regulations in relation to children.

The field of children's consumerism can be approached as a social construction to which several institutions contribute, such as consultants, industrials, governmental bodies, families, media etc. As the field is embedded in the abovementioned sub-systems, actions aimed at selling and marketing products to children are very complex.

This is further developed by the author, who gives advice to managers addressing children as a segment. The importance of the ethical perspective when marketing to children is underlined. For instance, some of the legal and ethical aspects of advertising to children are presented with reference – among others – to some of the initiatives of the European Commission.

The chapter concludes by highlighting the need for socially responsible research, which implies two major shifts, i.e. an inter-disciplinary dialogue in research processes and a willingness to engage in discussions about the ethical ground on which the theoretical frameworks are based.

In the eighth chapter of the book, Children as Change Agents in the Pursuit of the Competencies of the Future, Anne Flemmert Jensen focuses on the challenges that await us concerning play and learning in the future. Fundamental changes are happening with our values and attitude towards play and learning, and this is affecting children's play practices and cultures as well as their learning styles. This will put new demands on educators and parents as well as companies targeting the children's market. In autumn 2003, the LEGO company conducted an international anthropological study of 8-14 year-olds' play practices and ways of talking about everyday lives. Some of the findings were that children look at the world very much the way adults do - a media and technology driven world, characterized by a large degree of individualism, fragmentation and diversity. However, rather than be concerned, children look more at the opportunities that the new world offers them. Other findings were that children paint a picture of a very individualistic society characterized by endless opportunities to reach personal and economic goals and that children are aware that freedom and responsibility are interlinked. One of the most frequent fears mentioned by the children was the fear of failure; not living up to the responsibility and expectations set by parents, school and society. The children also showed an interest in not merely acquiring knowledge and information but learning things in a meaningful and playful context. Jensen uses the study to question the return to a more traditionalist form of education, which is currently being contemplated by some politicians in some Northern European countries. She suggests that we instead should start listening to the children and learn from their approach to everyday life.

References

Brembeck, H. et al. (ed.) (2005); *Beyond the competent child*. Roskilde University Press.

Brembeck, H. and B. Johansson (ed.) (1996); *Postmodern barndom.* Göteborg: Etnologiska föreningen i Västsverige.

Buckingham, D. (2000); *After the death of childhood – growing up in the age of electronic media*. Cambridge: Polity Press.

Christensen, Ole and Birgitte Tufte (2001); *Familier i forandring – hverdag og medier i danske familier*. Copenhagen: Akademisk Forlag.

La Ville (de), V. I. (ed.) (2005); *L'enfant consommateur. Variations interdisciplinaires sur l'enfanct et le marché*. France: Institut Vital Roux.

Gunter, B. and A. Furnham (1997); *Children as Consumers. A psychological analysis of the young people's market*. London and New York: Routledge.

James, A., C. Jenks and A. Prout (1998); *Theorizing Childhood*. Cambridge: Polity Press.

Johansson, B. (2000); *Kom och ät! Jag ska bara dö först. Datorn i barns vardag*. Göteborg: Etnologiske föreningen I Västsverige.

Kampmann, J. (2005): Societalization of Childhood: New Opportunities? New Demands? in H. Brembeck, et al. (ed.), *Beyond the competent child*. Roskilde University Press.

Kenway, J. and E. Bullen (2001/2003); *Consuming Children – Education – entertainment – advertising*. Maidenhead, Philadelphia: Open University Press.

Kinder, M. (1999) (ed.); *Kids Media Culture*. Duke University Press.

Kline, S. et al. (2003); *Digital Play. The Interaction of Technology, Culture, and Marketing*. Quebec City: McGill-Queens' University Press.

Kline, S. (1993); *Out of the Garden. Toys, TV, and Children's Culture in the Age of Marketing*. London, New York: VERSO.

Livingstone, S. et al. (2004); *Active participation or just more information – young people's take up of opportunities to act and interact on the internet*. A research report from the UK Children Go Online project.
http:www.children-go-online.net

Livingstone, S. & M. Bovill (2001); *Children and Their Changing Media Environment. A European Comparative Study*. London: Lawrence Erlbaum Associates, Publishers.

McNeal, J.U. (1992); *Kids as customers: A handbook of marketing to children*. New York: Lexington Books.

Tufte, Birgitte, Jeanette Rasmussen and Lars Pynt Andersen (2004-2006); *Tweens between Media and Consumption*. Ongoing research project regarding the role of new media in 10-12 year-old children's consumption. About the project see (in Danish) B. Tufte in *Humaniora,* No. 4, 2004. Copenhagen.

Tufte, Birgitte (2003); Children, media and consumption in *International Journal of Advertising & Marketing to Children, Vol 5., Issue 1*. World Advertising Research Centre.

1

Understanding and Theorizing Modern Childhood in Denmark: Tendencies and Challenges

JAN KAMPMANN

Researching, understanding and theorizing modern childhood has been a form of academic endeavour that has increased dramatically during the last 10-15 years. Not only in a Danish context, but in an international perspective, this has resulted in pools of knowledge and piles of publications[1]. Part of this widespread work has focused on how children seemingly have changed, other contributions have been more interested in highlighting how the conditions of modern childhood have undergone crucial ruptures and developments, while some contributions have been more interested in showing that it is the understanding of and approach to children that has changed. There is probably no doubt that all three perspectives could be said to point to central issues, and a proper treatment would have to explore more deeply how those three dimensions mutually shape each other. In this chapter, I will confine myself to a brief description of these dimensions, in the hope of providing a point of departure for further critical debates.

Children and the welfare state: From private to shared responsibility

Historically, the child has been in the domain of the family. This was the case during the 19th century, irrespective of whether the view on

---

[1] An overview and critical discussion of extensive parts of this work is presented in Kampmann, 2003.

the child was as a producer, an expense or a human being in need of care. This view gradually changed during the course of the 20th century, meaning that the child has become more the focus of a shared or cooperative project between parents and the welfare state; a project that has become increasingly ambitious.

Essential elements in this development are the introduction of compulsory school attendance, free admission to state schools, and from 1919 the introduction of public funding for establishing and running childcare institutions. Subsequently important developments, such as the extension of childcare services for all children, including babies as well as school children, and the introduction of maternity leave, have all had an impact.

For many years, the demand for full coverage was the central issue in the daycare debate. This goal could be said to have been reached during the 1990s.

Following the tendency that most parents – both fathers and mothers – are engaged in the labour market, there has been a very dramatic development regarding the number of places for children in the public daycare facilities.

Table 1:1. Children attending public daycare facilities, coverage rates, 1973-2000 (%)

	1973	1979	1985	1990	1995	2000
0-2 years	16	29	42	47	48	56
3-5 years	35	51	67	76	82	92

Source: Bonke, 1997: 388; Børns levevilkår, 2002: 105

In 1999, a more comprehensive picture of all children (aged six months to nine years) attendance at public daycare facilities was as seen in Table 1:2.

This indicates clearly that at present there is more or less full access for children of pre-school age. Especially when we examine the age group three to five years, we can see that around 91% of all children are in some form of public daycare facility – even though it is not compulsory.[2]

Compared to other EU Member States, it seems to be of vital importance that the Danish public daycare facilities fall under the auspices of the Ministry of Social Affairs and not under the Ministry of Education. Furthermore, the staff in these different institutional

---

[2] For further elaboration on this issue, see Kampmann and Nielsen, 2004.

settings are not called 'pre-schoolteachers' and the like (and have therefore no immediate rhetorical link to the education system), but are primarily called 'pedagogues'[3] (with three and a half years of full-time training), childminders and 'nursery and childcare assistants', the latter being employees without a full and relevant qualification.

Table 1:2. Coverage for children aged six months to nine years enrolled in daycare facilities, April 1999 (%)

	Childminder arrangement	Crèche	Kindergarten	Age-integrated facility	After-school centre, SFO and club	Total
0.5-2 years	41	10	1	12	0	64
3-5 years	6	1	51	31	1	91
6-9 years	0	0	6	11	63	81
0.5-9 years	13	3	19	18	27	80

Source: Ministry of Social Affairs, 2000:25.

In the last few years, more interest has been directed towards the opening hours of the daycare institutions, and the most recent elements in this development are an extension of maternity leave, the introduction of parental leave and the introduction of user boards in daycare institutions and schools. These elements have been combined with attempts to increase the influence of state and local authorities on the pedagogy applied in daycare institutions and schools. As a new 'invention' in the Danish context, all public daycare institutions are required to work in accordance with a nationally defined curriculum.

This new interest shown in the welfare system has been accompanied by a similar growing concern about Children at Risk, social deprivation and negative social inheritance. In line with this, it is apparent that public daycare facilities are seen as a central part of the welfare services; a part that has been ascribed the function of changing and improving the situation. Not least the political and governmental systems are very keen to see public daycare facilities implementing, or at least testing, different kinds of compensatory pedagogic activities, aimed at bettering the situation for Children at Risk, etc. (see, for

---

[3] The training programme to become a teacher and the training programme to become a pedagogue are still separated and situated in different 'colleges' (seminarier), which again are both separated from university studies and the university institution. However, it must be said that at the moment there seems to be a huge political interest in reforming and restructuring the whole system.

example, Ministerudvalget for negativ social arv og social mobilitet 2003).

The last few years have seen an extraordinary interest in establishing a pool of knowledge about the possibilities and abilities of the school and daycare institution to compensate and prevent negative social inheritance, social deprivation and children becoming Children at Risk (Bayer and Ellegaard, 1999; Christensen, 1996; Christensen and Egelund, 2002; Hansen, 1999; Hestbæk and Christoffersen, 2002; Jensen and Jørgensen, 1999; Jensen, Barrett and Christoffersen, 2003; Ringsmose, Nielsen and Fink-Jensen, 2003). Furthermore, there has been an acute interest in how social policy and social pedagogic initiatives can contribute to empowering children's lives and to improving their learning and their life skills in such a way as to contribute to the 'breaking of the law of social inheritance' or to compensate for some children's social deprivation and situation as Children at Risk (Jensen, Barrett and Christoffersen, 2003; Ellegaard and Stanek, 2004).

In a more general perspective, this kind of public involvement can be perceived as a sign of the qualitatively heightened level of welfare intervention with respect to children.

Children as political subjects

The political status and position that children are ascribed in a broader societal context, as seen through legislation and practices of governance and more locally in connection with the position of pupils at a given school, in organizations and even in their families, has in a similar vein changed dramatically during the last 10-15 years. Such a shift in the way society and the general public perceive children and childhood is without doubt closely connected to the Danish parliament's ratification of the UN Convention on the Rights of the Child in 1991. Initially, however, the UN Convention was largely ignored in Denmark, which was quite the opposite to what was seen in, for instance, Norway. Despite the neglect of the UN Convention, a profound rupture in the perception of children could be detected. It was seen in the basic understanding of, the approach to, and the respect for the individual child, children and childhood. This was very much explicated through new rhetoric, implying that children should be seen as 'beings in their own right', 'as having agency', and 'of being competent'. This new rhetoric was obviously tied to certain progressive pedagogic movements and childhood studies, research and the like, but at the same time it was part of a much broader trend, which could be seen in public opinion, in the media and among parents. The 1990s can be seen as a decade where a growing will to recognize children and children's rights was apparent. The evolution of new forms of administration in cases relating to children resulted in children being involved and heard, often at a younger age than seen before, and in cases of placement after divorce, removal from parental care (with or without consent) and so forth.

In schools, a continuation of these inclusionary processes focused on building up democratic councils and bodies, such as boards involving parents, increased parental and pupil inclusion in school assemblies, pupil associations consisting of pupil representatives from each class in the school, and 'Klassens time' (The Hour of the Class), where all pupils in the specific class would have the right and opportunity to participate in discussions and decisions. In Denmark, such initiatives were not entirely new nor the result or consequence of the UN Convention. In fact, there have been experiments and experiences concerning different kinds of democratic practice in state schools for a number of years. One interpretation would be that the UN Convention in the Danish context was initially seen as a much needed and necessary initiative for the sake of children in *other* countries, especially in the 'Third World'. Nevertheless, it seems that in the second half of the 1990s, the UN Convention on the Rights of the Child began to have an impact in the Danish context. This means that earlier critique and questioning of the 'hegemonic discourse', saying that children should be seen as competent participants in democratic processes, could, with reference to the UN Convention, be interpreted not as a question of ideology, but fundamentally as a societal, administrative and legally defined right that children and childhood were assigned.

Approaching the new millennium, the debates, discussions, understandings and interest in children seemed to increase further in the public sphere, and there emerged a much more explicit and continuous reference to the UN Convention as the foundation on which policy, governance, pedagogy and daily practice in families as well as institutions should be built. Instead of understanding the UN Convention as an ideological document, it became increasingly interpreted as the legislative document it is. This implies that the discussion concerning children's rights, the principles guiding different kinds of practice involving children, etc. were not only founded on pedagogic or psychological arguments, as they previously were, but on political and legal considerations as well, signalling a very important step forward for children towards gaining a new position as co-citizens.

In organizations, such as the National Council for Children (Børnerådet) and Children's Conditions (Børns Vilkår), as well as in schools, daycare settings and public administrations, there is clearly a tendency to focus on the implications of UN Convention's democratic and participatory rights. One central element in this new agenda is the need and obligation to look at children not only as subjects with individual rights, but also as a socially definable group with specific common interests which they have the right to declare. Furthermore, children can expect that they will be listened to, and that their opinions will have weight in decision-making. The fact that children are now seen as a group with, to an extent, common interests underlines the need to qualify attempts to more fully understand and perceive how and what children are trying to express - about their concerns, their understanding of themselves and the world around them - through their daily agency, negotiations and meaning-making processes. Due to the differences in how children and adults are socially positioned, attempts have been made to construct a 'child perspective' – in research as well as in the pedagogic and political debate (Kampmann, 1998).

There is no doubt that this leads to a degree of 'political correctness', whereby the vocabulary developed by professionals and experts becomes increasingly used and disseminated through public debates and the media. Everyone is expected to do their best to understand what children are trying to communicate, which again seems to strengthen a certain understanding of children as 'able' – able to act, to interact, to communicate, to establish meaning, to negotiate and to make choices – in a Danish rhetoric very often comprised in the term 'the competent child' (Juul, 1996). In the case of the child in the family, the competent child has been combined with an understanding of the 'negotiating family', indicating that the positions of children and parents have undergone crucial changes, resulting in family practices where children are invited and expected to participate in daily negotiations concerning meals, bed-times, clothing, media consumption, etc.

In this very abstract, generalized and, in some respects, idealized approach to and understanding of children, we see an interesting ambiguity, related to what could be called a specific 'zeitgeist':

On the one hand, we can identify a kind of cultural release of children, whereby the respect for children's interests, their democratic rights, their choices and ways of dealing with each other and the world clearly offers them a space for agency and independence that has not been seen on this scale before. Children are given the opportunity to have their say and are deemed to have agency in a seemingly very comprehensive and extensive way. As mentioned, this is seen as a democratic right, more than as a necessity in pedagogic or psychological terms, which of course is not an overnight shift of emphasis or a change fuelled by the UN Convention. Rather, it must be seen as tightly woven into the overall modernization of the Danish society; a process that has occurred over decades and can be said to express a qualitatively new crystallization of ongoing generational processes and shifting power relations between children and adults (Alanen, 2000 and 2001).

On the other hand, we might consider these new approaches and initiatives targeting children and 'modern childhood(s)' as an increased 'pedagogization of children's life' (Bernstein, 2001), meaning that there appears to be an increasing number of new demands and expectations towards children, not only in daycare and school settings, but in the public sphere as well.

The 'schoolification' of children

Instead of teachers, pedagogues and parents explicitly defining rules and regulations, children are expected to act in accordance with the cultural codes. 'The competent child' in this perspective would also imply that the child, on its own initiative, acts in accordance with the expectations of parents or professionals without them having the need to explicate these expectations. The child might be said to be self-determining, but only in a specific and narrow sense: determining within the bounds of what is expected. This kind of self-imposed decision-making and responsibility could also be said to be the case when we consider children's learning processes in school settings and the like. It is increasingly the case that there is a defined pedagogic attitude towards children's learning which states that they are supposed to be 'responsible for own learning'. The 'good pupil' is therefore the one that by his or her own initiative determines to work with this or that content, in this or that manner, expecting to reach this or that goal by including these and those methods and materials. This kind of self-imposed responsibility for your own learning could be seen as a new 'technology of the self' in a foucauldian sense, as a way of installing new types of governance and productive discipline based on governmentality – the ability and openness to be governed mainly by doing what is expected, without any need for using visible power or explicitly being forced to it (Foucault, 1991; Rose, 1996).

To establish an understanding of these ruptures and breaks in the attitude and approach to the self-determining *and* responsible pupil, Lynn Fendler talks about the need for understanding children and pupils in terms of developmentalism and interactionism, and at the same time points to the possible effect that the pedagogic devices are more focused on *governing the soul* than on *disciplining the body* or *training the intellect* (Fendler, 1999: 185). This tendency is reflected in the 1993 Education Act, which focuses on what is termed 'pupil-differentiated teaching', meaning the need for an individualized curriculum, involving the pupil in decisions about what to work with and study, in what manner and at what pace. To be 'responsible for own learning' includes techniques such as portfolios, logbooks, the child's book, etc., which all, in different ways, imply the active involvement, choice and decision making by the child itself. Similarly, it is now normal procedure for the child or maybe a group of children to be involved in a kind of formative or 'running' evaluation and assessment of their achievements. As part of this ongoing self-evaluation, it is common in many schools to use a 'conversation sheet'. Prior to meetings between the teacher, the pupil and the pupil's parents, the pupil is expected to fill in the sheet by making evaluative comments on where he/she feels secure/insecure, where he/she ought to improve, where he/she sees coming challenges and what to do about them etc. This example clearly demonstrates that the child is supposed to think and work in accordance to a specific rationality which is defined not by the child as part of its self-determination, but is predefined in line with the logic and wishes of the school. This again illustrates that everyday practices in schools must be seen as based on power relations, even when these relations seem to be more invisible than before (Bernstein 1996). The power relations between teachers and pupils are not diminishing or vanishing; rather they are reconstructed and restructured as part of an ongoing modernization of conditions related to childhood.

As indicated, this should not only be regarded as a new phenomenon in Danish schools, but also as a very significant element in practice in daycare institutions as well. Working with 'the child's book' starts in the daycare facilities, or otherwise the staff will work with each child having its 'suitcase', loaded with personal tracks and stories, where these staff will be working hard to document the individual child's performance and achievement (Cecchin, 1998). Additionally, staff will probably adopt a kind of 'step-by-step' method, taking seriously children's own responsibility when it comes to dealing and coping with - and especially resolving – conflicts.

It could be said that in Danish schools and daycare facilities the pedagogic winds are blowing in the direction of encouraging children to play an active role in their own socialization process, in their social inclusion, in their own discipline and/or in their acquisition of abilities, competences and qualifications – depending on how we wish to interpret these new trends.

At any rate, what is common for the new technologies of the self in schools and daycare settings is the expectation that the child is willing, able and skilled in talking about itself – making confessions as a voluntarily agreed upon everyday practice. Instead of a pedagogic practice built on the inspection carried out by the pedagogue, we can see a new kind of pedagogic practice in the form of an introspection performed by the child itself.

The pedagogic colonization of children's lives in school and daycare should in many respects be seen as new, but nonetheless they are related to known conceptions and practices. The demands placed on children to be self-responsible through some degree of self-determination can be seen as founded in the idea about the 'naturally developing child' (James, Jenks and Prout, 1998). The child is seen as having a natural interest in and ability to take on and direct itself towards the demands for self-regulation.

This issue, the child's right to self-determination, shows that there are conflicting interpretations depending on how we analyse and assess the contemporary conditions, intentions and practices. Without any doubt, this discussion about children's self-determination and their 'responsibility for own learning' must be seen as crucial for understanding some of the important contemporary debates and discussions concerning childhood in Denmark. But equally important, the issue must be seen as an indicator for understanding contemporary conditions for being a child in Denmark. The logic and rationality of 'responsible and sensible' self-determination has impact on the structuring of children's access to and use of time and space; and vice-versa, children's social and economic situation and condition offers very diverse opportunities for experiencing self-determination as freedom, as a burden, as part of reality or an illusion, as something they can cope with, or demands they are not able to grasp or in a position to do anything about.

Institutionalized individualization and individualized institutionalization

Children's everyday lives both in and outside of institutions (daycare facilities, schools, sports clubs, families, etc.) can as a consequence be seen increasingly to be organized in accordance with an ambiguous rationality. On the one hand, it is publicly declared that children should be and are seen as individuals with individual rights, having both a say and the freedom to negotiate their own wishes, interests and identity. In the words of the German sociologist, Ulrick Beck, it can be seen as the possibility *and* the demand for individualization (Beck and Beck-Gernsheim, 2002). On the other hand, it can be argued that children in Denmark are expected very early in their life to attend and participate in public daycare facilities in order to be 'normally socialized', or socialized to be a 'normal child'. It seems to be the case that in the Danish context the appropriate normalizing and social inclusionary practice emphasizes increased participation in the public socializing system – in welfare institutional settings.

At first, from the beginning of the 1990s, this was explicitly said in relation to bilingual children, when several Danish municipalities initiated different forms of out-reach work for the families with an ethnic minority background who had not of their own accord enrolled their child in an official daycare facility when the child was three years old. At first, the reason given to the families was that this was to create an opportunity for their child to take advantage of the pedagogic activities in the institution, especially with regard to picking up the language, which afterwards would strengthen their chances of subsequently beginning school on equal terms with 'other' children. But another argument became increasingly used, namely that it was on the whole appropriate and almost essential to be part of a daycare environment if one was to acquire the necessary cultural, social and personal competences and skills, not just to do well in school, but to do well at all.

In recent years, this has become so universal and further strengthened that, as mentioned, it has been decided on a national level to introduce curricula in all daycare institutions on the basis of a centrally determined framework for a national curriculum. Within this framework, it is up to the individual municipality, and within these up to the individual institution, to decide how specifically to fill out this framework. However, the interesting point is that an important aspect of the demands to the curriculum in the framework is targeted at enhancing the child's development of personal characteristics and competences. The fact that a national curriculum has been introduced just increases the tendency towards a welfare state socialization of children, where their fundamental personality formation is seen as an essential element in those areas of a child's growth and development that fall within the realm of local and state institutions. The individualization process as a real life history process phenomenon seems in a basic sense in the Danish context to be interwoven with the functions ascribed to the institution system. In this way, it becomes to an increasing degree regarded as *a matter of course that individualization is institutionalized.*

On the other hand, it is possible to observe an equally interesting movement in the form of *the individualization of the institution.* In the Danish context, this can be said to be founded in the widespread pedagogic declaration of taking the point of departure in 'the individual child'; a new rhetoric which gradually becomes an increasingly integrated part of the various forms of pedagogic and didactic development and new formulations during the 1990s. Not just in the context of daycare institutions, but also to a great extent in the school, more and more pedagogic ideas and concrete forms of practice are developed which emphasize the individual child's and the individual pupil's actions and own responsibility. As mentioned, there is a general dissemination of pedagogic work and activity forms, where it is the individual child who must create its individual 'line'. The child must voice its individual interests and inquisitiveness, learn to be explicit about its own individual feelings, develop its own individual ways to handle its wishes and choices, take responsibility for the role it plays as an individual in conflicts and thereby also in their resolution keep its personal and individual logbook or portfolio. Lastly, the child must voice its expectations to and play an active role in the planning of its own individual learning processes; first by addressing what has to be worked with specifically and in what ways, and then by conducting (self-)evaluation, which involves a critical analysis of what one as an individual pupil did well or badly, what can be improved etc.

On the rhetorical level, this is underpinned by the increasing attention to and active involvement of the UN Convention on the

Rights of the Child, where, in principle, in a similar way, the emphasis is primarily on the formulations about the right of the individual child to be heard, to participate and to make decisions.

Altogether, one can point at an intense implementation of the individualization perspective with the related idea of the personally and individually reflective and competent child.

New 'ideals of normality'

In continuation of the widespread societal expectation that the development of the individual child's personality formation and thereby its individualization process are linked to the official institutional system, as well as in continuation of the increased tendency that the point of departure for activity and learning considerations is the individual child/pupil or the single individual, new conditions for the social inclusion processes can be detected. Naturally, these processes are correspondingly accompanied by new conditions and forms of exclusionary processes. In other words, a basis seems to be established for a new form of normalization practice, where individualization and focus on the individual child are not only a release and an extension of the individual's room to manoeuvre, but also constitute the foundation for demands made on the child with accompanying assessment and evaluation criteria. The children and the pupils are expected to be responsible for their own learning and individualization to such an extent that this makes up an essential element in the basis of what is increasingly regarded as *expectable*, *desirable* and *achievable*, i.e what can be considered as *normal* in relation to the individual child's development and daily performance. This implies a special form of expectation that the individual child should be able to 'control itself' – to establish a form of 'self-governance' – and thereby in many ways, on its own initiative and according to its own impulse, be rational, sensible and, on the whole, 'un-childish'. On the other hand, what we have seen are not demands and requirements that are particularly explicit, but rather, as previously touched on, can be understood in the light of the tendency pointed out by Bernstein to develop an invisible pedagogy.

The demand is thus not only that the individual child is expected to control itself, but to control itself without being explicitly told to do so! In other words, the child, as part of the normalization demand, is expected to be able to 'break the code', and thereby sense what is demanded in the specific situation. The optimal in this new form of normalization practice would be for the individual child, on its own, to make the choices of activities, forms of action and ways of being that are expected by the adults, but to do so partly without being instructed to by adults, and partly so that the individual child feels such action to be in accordance with precisely what it wanted itself and felt inclined to do itself.

Conversely, it means that the children who cannot similarly make these choices and do these forms of self-initiated actions, in principle risk exclusion and marginalization. Or seen from the perspective of the pedagogic institution, they marginalize themselves, in that it is basically understood as an expression of the individual child's and the individual pupil's own choice. The responsibility for not only the integrative, but conversely also for the excluding processes is attributed to a great extent to children and pupils themselves – not on the basis of intelligence and abilities, but on the basis of their individuality and personal competences – and their willingness!

The competent child as compulsive idea

These observations also create a new basis for understanding the nature of the competent Danish child. One could presume that the strength of this concept could be connected with social-scientifically based circumscriptions of the fact that Danish children display a demonstrably and recordable increased degree of competent behaviour or can, in a measurable way, express themselves more competently than previously seen, registered and measured. However, this is in no way the most important point in the use of the concept of the competent child. There are probably no scientific studies that can say anything substantial or definitive about whether or not such changes have occurred. The point is probably rather that the competent child is a projection of a certain idea about how children in a particular Danish welfare state, in a reflective and democratically oriented societal and cultural context, are expected to be able to act. The competent element has thus primarily a signal value, as it signals a new childhood ideal, a new normativity and declared approach to children, which is probably more a reflection of a value standard than it is necessarily a descriptive category that records what 'the Danish child' is like, on the basis of scientific material. Rather, it records how to an increasing extent there are some collective ideas and ideal notions about what 'the Danish child' *should* be like. Thus, there is a certain degree of a compulsive idea, in the sense that there increasingly seems to be a form of shared idea among politicians, pedagogic experts and professionals, as well as parents, that children *are* competent, which conversely means that those who in various ways are deemed not to be competent constitute a problem, because they, as it were, are sub-normal – i.e under the expectable standard.

Children now, through the UN convention, through pedagogic initiatives and through a growing 'negotiation culture' in the family etc., are more and more respected as beings and not just becomings, as individuals with rights who should be listened to and with whom decisions should be made. Concurrently, there is also a parallel movement, where the development if anything can be described as making ever-increasing demands on children at an ever earlier stage in their life. And rather than speaking about a liberation of children and childhood, one can at least critically ask if it is not just as much a case of an extended form of pedagogically reflected sequestration of childhood.

Persisting ambiguities in modern childhood

In any discussion or assessment of modern Danish childhood, it is important to stress the very ambivalent and dichotomous developmental trends that can be identified.

In my account, I have weighted the presentation of the ruptures and changes as relatively unequivocal and one-dimensional with regard to their developmental direction, almost without inner difficulties, inconsistencies and conflicts. Maybe this can be said to be very much in accordance with other contributions to this volume, where children are seen as powerful, skilled and competent consumers, as reasonable and authoritative agents in the area of the new communication technologies, as more and more visible and forming their own 'segment' for those working with marketing, etc.

It is important to approach this position at least along two lines:
On the one hand, it can be important to point out circumstances that perhaps pull just as much in other directions. Thus there are clearly important forces that are fighting to (re-)introduce clearer and more explicit professional goals, formulated in traditional single-discipline terms more than in personal and social competence terms. These forces are also riding on the crest of a wave with regard to demanding a form

of rehabilitation of the adults' authority and a more unequivocal power position as those responsible for what children should do in their institutional and non-institutional everyday context.

The counter-movements can also be interpreted as more defensive attempts to handle new and in many ways both confusing and anxiety-provoking types of demands and requirements. Because, as already mentioned, changes in the ideas and practice about and requirements for children through changed generationing processes mean that correspondingly, new and quite far-reaching demands and requirements are made for being an adult, whether it is as a parent or as a professional. Some of the current initiatives from groups of parents, politicians, administrative personnel and teachers/educationists - where the aim is to re-establish a visible pedagogy, unequivocal adult expertise, discipline, control and responsibility - can be understood as pure self-defence against being confronted with expectations about being able to grasp completely different types of understandings and practice forms in relation to children, thus as an almost desperate attempt to re-introduce 'the good old days', when a child was a child, an adult was an adult, and the difference could be defined, understood and felt.

On the other hand, we can interpret the growing focus on respecting, listening and giving responsibility to the so-called 'competent child' as part of another kind of ongoing struggle between two different kinds of 'modernization interests'. There are surely quite a number of adults, parents as well as professionals that are very sincere about the project of giving voice to children, letting them have a say, and contributing to the empowerment of this group of people, which hitherto can be said to have suffered by a lack of access to democratic participation concerning matters related to their own everyday life. Part of this chapter can be said to expose the kind of understanding where children as individuals and as a group are seen as being equipped with increased power and democratic rights.

In opposition to the interpretation pointing to new democratic rights, another part of the chapter can be said to contribute to a construction and interpretation where the changes and developments are understood as signalling an extensive and intensive colonization of childhood. The seemingly increased interest in exposing children as able and competent is merely a blurring of distinctions between being a child, a young person and being adult, which mirrors the basic interest in inscribing children (and young people) in the general principles of corporate cultural logics, demands and aims. Children's everyday life is not only (re-)structured by the aforementioned increased quantitative and qualitative grounded institutionalization, but as well by the marketization of childhood, pointing not as much to children's position as being and becoming citizens, but more narrowly as consumers and agents on the market.

It should be an ongoing concern to discuss whether this kind of modernization points to a genuine empowerment of children. And it should furthermore be discussed what empowerment of children actually entails!

References

Alanen, L. (2000); Childhood as a generational condition. Towards a relational theory of childhood, in J. Olesen, N. de Coninck-Smith, F. Mouritsen and J. Qvortrup (eds.), *Research in Childhood. Sociology, Culture and History. A collection of Papers*. Odense: University of Southern Denmark.

Alanen, L. (2001); Explorations in generational analysis, in L. Alanen and B. Mayall (eds.), *Conceptualizing Child-Adult Relations*. London: RoutledgeFalmer Press.

Bayer, S. and T. Ellegaard (1999); *Den sociale arv set i forhold til det fysiske miljø og daginstitutionerne*. Working Paper 24 om social arv. Copenhagen: Socialforskningsinstituttet.

Beck, U. and E. Beck-Gernsheim (2002); *Individualization: Institutionalized individualism and its social and political consequences*. London: Sage Publications.

Bernstein, B. (1996); *Pedagogy, Symbolic Control and Identity: Theory, Research, Critique*. London: Taylor and Francis.

Bernstein, B. (2001); Dialogue, in A. Morais et al. (eds.), *Towards a Sociology of Pedagogy: The Contribution of Basil Bernstein to Research*. New York: Peter Lang Publication.

Bonke, J. (ed.) (1997); *Levevilkår I Danmark 1997*. Copenhagen: Danmarks Statistik/Socialforskningsinstituttet.

Børns Levevilkår (2002); *Børns levevilkår*. Copenhagen: Danmarks Statistik.

Cecchin, D. (1998); *Den integrerende baggrund*. Copenhagen: Forlaget Børn & Unge.

Christensen, E. (1996); *Daginstitutionen som forebyggende tilbud til truede børn*. Copenhagen: Socialforskningsinstituttet.

Christensen, E. and T. Egelund (2002); *Børnesager. Evaluering af den forebyggende indsats*. Copenhagen: Socialforskningsinstituttet.

Ellegaard, T. and A.H. Stanek (eds.) (2004); *Læreplaner i børnehaven. Baggrund og perspektiver*. Frederiksberg: Roskilde Universitetsforlag.

Fendler, L. (1999); Making Trouble: prediction, agency, and critical intellectuals, in T.S. Popkewitz and L. Fendler (eds.), *Critical Theories in Education*. London: Routledge.

Foucault, M. (1991); Governmentality, in G. Burchell, C. Gordon and P. Miller (eds.), *The Foucault Effect. Studies in Governmentality*. Chicago: University of Chicago Press.

Hansen, E.J. (1999); *Social arv og uddannelse*. Working Paper 22 om social arv. Copenhagen: Socialforskningsinstituttet.

Hestbæk, A.-D. and M.N. Christoffersen (2002); *Effekter af børnepasning – en redegørelse for nationale og internationale forskningsresultater*. Working paper. Copenhagen: Socialforskningsinstituttet.

James, A., C. Jenks and A. Prout (1998); *Theorizing Childhood*. Cambridge and Oxford: Polity Press.

Jensen, B. and P.S. Jørgensen (1999); *Social arv og competence – bidrag til en model*. Working Paper 5 om social arv. Copenhagen: Socialforskningsinstituttet.

Jensen, B., B.A. Barrett and M.N. Christoffersen (2003); *Daginstitutioner som instrument til at bryde social arv – hvad ved vi fra den nationale og internationale forskning og hvad gør vi?* Working

Paper 8, Vidensopsamlingen om social arv 2003. Copenhagen: Socialforskningsinstituttet.

Juul, J. (1996); *Dit kompetente barn.* Copenhagen: Schønbergs Forlag.

Kampmann, J. (1998); *Børneperspektiv og børn som informanter.* Copenhagen: Børnerådet.

Kampmann, J. (2003); Barndomssociologi – fra marginaliseret provokatør til mainstream leverandør, in *Dansk Sociologi,* no.2, vol.14.

Kampmann, J. and H.W. Nielsen (2004); Socialized Childhood: Children's Childhoods in Denmark, in A.-M. Jensen, B.A. Asher, C. Conti, D. Kutsar, M.N.G. Phádraig and H.W. Nielsen (eds.), *Children's Welfare in Ageing Europe.* Vol.2. Trondheim: COST/Norsk senter for barneforskning.

Ministerudvalget for negative social arv og social mobilitet (2003); *En god start til alle børn.* Copenhagen: Socialministeriet.

Ministry of Social Affairs (2000); *Early Childhood Education and Care Policy in Denmark. Background Report. OECD Thematic Review of Early Childhood Education and Care Policy.* Copenhagen: The Ministry of Social Affairs.

Ringsmose, C., A.M. Nielsen and K. Fink-Jensen (2003); *Skolen som instrument til at bryde den negative sociale arv.* Working Paper 9, Vidensopsamlingen om social arv. Copenhagen: Socialforskningsinstituttet.

Rose, N. (1996); *Inventing Our Selves.* London: Sage Publication.

2

Children as Innovators and Opinion Leaders

FLEMMING HANSEN AND
MORTEN HALLUM HANSEN

Background

In contemporary studies of children's socialization as consumers, emphasis is put on their use of mass media. Their possession of audio/visual equipment such as televisions, videos, stereos and walkmans is in focus (Bejot et al., 2004; Geraci and Nagy, 2004; Feilitzen, 2002; Hansen et al., 2002a, 2002b). Also their access to electronic media, such as computers, game consoles, mobile phones, photo or printing equipment, attracts considerable interest (Tufte, 2003).

In this concern with electronic media, the role of personal communication among the children as well as between children and adults tends to be overlooked, and so does the role children play as innovators. In some markets, they are among the very first adopters. This applies to mobile phones, video games, etc. In others, they are by and large the only adopters. This applies to products such as Pokemon, Harry Potter, LEGO games, etc. Moreover to the child, at one point in time, all consumer products are new. At a certain time, the child for the first time meets Coca-Cola, cheese, sports shoes, bikes, etc. Some children do so before others and in the process they learn from each other.

A theoretical framework which has proven useful in the study of the role of different information sources, mass as well as personal, for the acceptance of new products, new habits, new behaviours etc., is the Diffusion of Innovations (Rogers, 1962, 1995). We shall first look at the extent to which we find the characteristics of 'Diffusion of Innovations' in children's behaviour when they learn about new products and behaviours. Particularly, we shall look at the role of opinion leaders and innovators among children. Before doing so, however, we shall review what the theory of 'Diffusion of Innovations' is all about, and ask what it means in a world with children adopting new products and behaviours

Next, we shall, with the use of qualitative as well as quantitative data, document the relevance of the diffusion of innovation theory in the study of children's socialization as consumers.

Following this, we shall focus on the opinion leaders and innovators among children. In this process, we shall look at the extent to which the characteristics of opinion leaders and innovators that have been found in general studies of Diffusion of Innovations among adults can be identified in the behaviour of children.

The Theory of Diffusion of Innovations

Diffusion of Innovations is concerned with acceptance of new practices, products and attitudes over time in a social system.

In this context, the term acceptance implies a decision process on behalf of the adopter much in line with general decision-making processes in the study of consumer behaviour. The term 'over time' implies that the acceptance is increasing with time in a particular way, characterized as the diffusion process, which is also to be dealt with in a subsequent section. In this process, the role of personal communication from such different categories as opinion leaders, gatekeepers, change agents, sales people, innovators and others are important.

In the following, we shall illustrate the adoption process, the innovation process and the form social influence may take among children maturing. In doing so, we shall draw upon data from a major study of Danish children growing up as consumers, reported in (Hansen et al., 2002a, 2002b), as well as qualitative observations from (Randrup and Lac, 2000).

Acceptance is seen as a process much like the general decision-making process on behalf of consumers (Nicosia, 1966; Howard and Sheth 1969; Hansen, 1972). The steps are:
- Awareness
- Interest
- Evaluation
- Test Purchase
- Adoption

In classical studies of diffusion of innovation, concern has been with, for instance, how farmers learn about new wheat sprays, how they through personal communication and media become interested in it, how they gather information, and how they eventually evaluate whether it is of interest for their own business or not. If so, then a trial takes place in a limited area of the land available for the farmer, and if this turns out positively, the use of the new wheat spray is eventually applied in the general running of the farm.

This process has been studied when consumers for the first time accept television, nylon stockings, ballpoint pens, home computers, etc. It is likely that the same occurs when children accept a new game, such as Pokemon, but also when they for the first time adopt new products, such as game consoles, mobile phones, etc.

Figure 2:1. The Growth in Awareness and Adoption – Iowa farmers' adoption of weed spray.

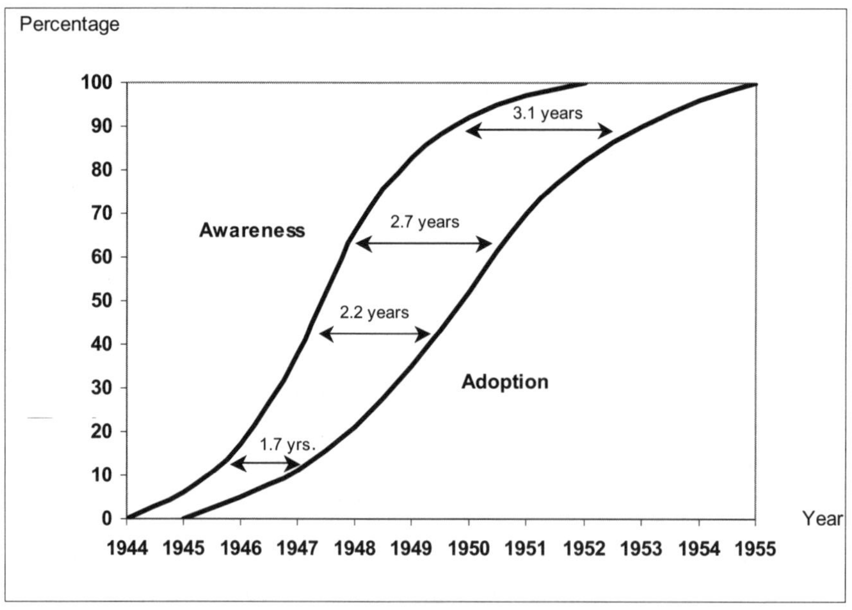

Adopted from: Rogers (1962, 1995) p. 200.

How the awareness of the innovation may arise is illustrated by a remark in our qualitative study by a Danish nine-year-old boy, who says (Randrup and Lac, 2000):

'Have you heard about the new thing in the USA, disposable mobile phones with one hour calling time. It cost about 300 DKK and then you have an hour calling time, but the price will probably come down quickly when it is no longer new.'

In the interest phase, the consumer seeks information. An eleven-year-old boy tells about mobile phones:

'It is stupid to ask in the store; they just want to sell the most expensive model. I trust my brother more.'

In another situation, a twelve-year-old boy talks about computer games:

'Because my big brother is a computer nerd, my big brother has most of the computer games.'

In the evaluation phase, the child combines its different information about the product and makes judgments: An eight-year-old girl answers:

'I don't want one now; my girlfriends don't have one, so what should I use it for.' (Leading to rejection)

About trial, an eight-year-old girl answers:

'I don't, but I've tried to play games on my mum or dad's computer – and I've also tried all my big sister's games.'

About acquisition of mobile phones, a nine-year-old boy says:

'I'm getting one; I may be getting my dad's old one when he buys a new one', and similarly an eight-year-old girl says about games: 'Yeah, but mostly I get games when someone in my family has a good game and then they burn a copy for me.'

Not all consumers adopt at the same time. It normally takes years before full penetration has been reached. In Figure 2:1, the typical growth in the possession or use of a new product is illustrated together with the way in which awareness of the existence of the new product develops. Initially, growth is slow, then it picks up, and when a majority of the consumers have adopted it, the growth rate drops. This diffusion process may last 20, 30 or 40 years, as has been the case with cars, telephones and other early major innovations. But it may also be fast, as has been the case with Hoola Hoop rings for children or the Che Guevara costume in the seventies.

In the study of diffusion of innovations, people are generally classified according to when they adopt the new product or practice. The typical grouping on the time dimension around which adoption takes place. The very first few (2.5%) are considered innovators, who are then followed by 13% early adopters. The majority is divided into early and late majority, constituting 68.5% of the total population, with 'laggards' making up the remaining 16%.

Particularly with children, this process may be seen in two different contexts. It may be seen with innovations where children are the only or the dominant adopters of the new behaviour, product or attitude. Barbie dolls and some video games are examples of the first. Mobile phones and CD players are other examples. Here, children are among the very early users of the new product.

In contrast with this, all that the child consumes is at one point in time new to the child. This applies to all existing products. When children and young people begin to use deodorants, cosmetics, shaving equipment, cola drinks, etc., one may look upon the different ages at which the children adopt the different products and expect an adoption process as described before to occur. Similarly, one may expect a diffusion process where the first users of mascara act as innovators, other girls as opinion leaders, and others plainly as followers.

Some examples of how innovations diffuse among children are the following. The percentage of Danish children who have a television in their own room grows from around 25% at the age of 5 to approximately 80% among the 15 to 18 year-olds. The possession of own Discman shows a coverage of around 60%. Finally, possession of own mobile phone is shown in Figure 2:2. Here, the rapid diffusion from around age 10 to age 14 is evident. The peculiar drop in coverage among the older children highlights as a special phenomenon that should be considered when studying innovations among children. Mobile phones became easily accessible in the early nineties. Data in Figure 2:2 are from a cross-sectional study in the year 2000. The children aged 15 at that time were very young at the beginning of the penetration of mobile phones in the 90's, and they did not manage to reach the maximum coverage before the year 2000. Later data show that the coverage rose to as high as 80–85%.

In a sense, the child's own room as an advanced electronic media centre may be seen as an innovation in itself. How this is developing with age is illustrated in Table 2:1. For most of the products, coverage has become high before the age of 13-15 years.

Figure 2:2. % Have own Mobile Phone

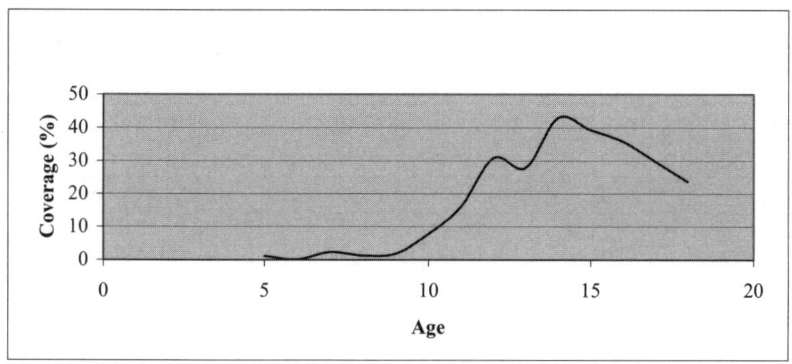

Table 2:1. Children in possession of own electronic media

Coverage in own room %	5-7 yrs.	8-10 yrs.	11-12 yrs.	13-15 yrs.	16-18 yrs
TV	38	50	64	72	76
Video	14	19	26	44	47
CD	21	28	27	35	38
Walkman	25	32	46	50	53
Discman	6	20	40	52	52
Playstation	13	25	25	19	10
PC	8	17	20	28	34
Printer	3	6	7	16	24

Also, a diffusion process can be observed in the development of daily consumption. This refers, for instance to the adoption of many food products, soft drinks, restaurant visits and personal care products. Data are shown in Table 2:2.

In contrast with the growing habits of regular use of soft drinks and fast food is the child's decreasing use of traditional food products, such as liver pâté, rye bread, etc. (Table 2:3). Here we may talk about de-learning. The consumption pattern is initially established by the parents. Following this, what happens may be seen as a case of negative innovation (Rogers, 1995), in the sense it reflects the children's decisions to 'not have' food habits forced upon them by their parents.

Table 2:2. Development in the consumption of products 'adopted'

Age	5	6	7	8	9	10	11	12	13	14	15	16	17	18	19-30
Food away from home	Consumption 1-3 times per month (%)														
Restaurant	7.4	8.3	12.5	7.7	6.6	10	14.1	15.7	11.6	13.6	18.4	16.7	21.6	22.1	30.3
Takeaway	13.6	7.3	10.2	10.3	9.6	13.9	17.2	16.3	16.3	25.0	23.3	31.7	27.7	28.2	27.9
Pizzeria	17.3	22.9	21.6	11.0	16.3	18.3	24.5	33.1	27.2	35.7	36.2	45.0	43.0	38.9	44.8
Sandwich bar	2.5	0.9	1.1	1.3	1.8	2.2	5.5	9.9	9.5	9.3	8.6	9.2	18.9	16.8	18.2
Personal care	Own choice products (%)														
Deodorant	3.7	--	5.7	4.5	10.8	17.8	42.3	62.8	75.5	86.4	88.3	89.2	91.9	90.8	89.9
Make-up	--	--	--	--	--	1.7	1.2	11.6	25.2	34.3	42.3	34.2	48.0	43.5	34.1
Soft drinks	Daily consumption (%)														
Soft drinks	6.2	7.3	5.7	4.5	6.6	8.9	10.4	12.2	18.4	11.4	19.0	24.2	18.2	31.3	21.7
Coca Cola	6.2	4.6	5.7	4.5	4.2	7.2	8.6	9.3	13.6	9.3	17.2	21.7	20.3	22.1	19.5

Table 2:3. Development in the consumption of products 'delearned'

Age	5	6	7	8	9	10	11	12	13	14	15	16	17	18	19-30
	Daily consumption (%)														
Liver pâte	37.0	40.4	30.7	32.3	33.1	30.0	23.9	22.1	17.7	13.6	12.3	17.5	12.2	16.0	13.8
Salami	34.6	26.6	23.9	24.5	26.5	20.0	17.2	15.1	12.9	4.3	6.1	10.0	7.4	6.9	7.7
Rye bread	93.8	92.7	93.2	89.7	86.7	80.6	80.4	77.9	63.9	59.3	58.9	55.8	61.5	63.4	56.1
Vitamin tablet	63.0	56.0	58.0	44.5	45.2	36.1	28.8	32.6	25.2	21.4	21.5	21.7	24.3	28.2	28.1

Finally we have cases where the child first adopts, and as it grows older the child again rejects such cases that may be labeled 'own choice', as illustrated in Table 2:4.

The way in which children's awareness of products and brands develops along the lines suggested in the first curve of Figure 2:1 can be seen from how brand awareness grows (Table 2:5).

Table 2:4. Development in the consumption of products own choice

Age	5	6	7	8	9	10	11	12	13	14	15	16	17	18	19-30
	Consumption 1-2 times per week (%)														
Liquorice	32.1	26.6	44.3	36.8	47.0	40.6	45.4	42.4	38.1	30.7	30.7	30.8	30.4	29.0	27.9
Nutella	18.5	4.6	19.3	28.4	28.9	19.4	28.8	24.4	9.5	3.6	6.1	9.2	6.1	3.1	3.2
Sweets	25.9	31.2	29.5	23.9	35.5	35.6	35.0	30.8	32.7	21.4	20.9	20.8	23.6	19.1	16.4

Table 2:5. Danish children's aided brand awareness

%	5-7 yrs.	8-10 yrs.	11-12 yrs.	13-15 yrs.	16-18 yrs.
Coca Cola	97	97	98	97	98
Cult	-	10	19	38	62
Kellogg's Cornflakes	95	96	98	97	97
OTA Guldkorn	73	75	62	63	69
Ericsson	21	50	86	92	94
Nokia	18	67	89	94	96
Motorola	8	32	65	79	84
Reebok	39	48	69	84	94
Puma	29	53	79	88	95

Children's awareness of individual brands for soft drinks and cereals are high already at an early age and does not change much as the child matures. Also the awareness of brand names in the area of sports shoes is quite high, but still increasing until around the age of 11-12 years. Finally, the awareness of mobile phone brand names increases all the way until the age of 16-18 years.

Social influence

In the generalized theory of Diffusion of Innovation, we find the following important characters:

- *Opinion leaders*, i.e. persons in the social environment from whom others take advice and whom they tend to copy in their behaviour.
- *Innovators*, i.e. those persons in the social group that accept the innovation first.
- *Gatekeepers*, i.e. those persons influencing the ability of the individual to adopt the innovation. Gatekeepers may be banks controlling the ability of farmers to adopt new technologies or, in

the world of the child, the parents making the acquisition of the innovation financially possible. The gatekeeper is described in the following statement made by a nine-year-old girl: 'It is only when the game needs to be inserted into the computer that my mother has to help me.'

- *Change agents, i.e.* normally persons outside the group providing information and advice of importance for the innovation in question. In the business community, this person may be a consultant. Among consumers, this person may be the private physician, a dietician or any other specialist. Among children, this person may be a schoolteacher or day care personnel.

Other important persons are *sales people*. Children to a large extent do their own shopping. That this is the case for selected products is shown in Table 2:6. They also visit stores frequently, as shown in Table 2:7.

Table 2:6. Children's own shopping

%	5-7 yrs.	8-10 yrs.	11-12 yrs.	13-15 yrs.	16-18 yrs.
Soft drinks / Coca Cola	2	3	12	27	45
Beer	--	--	--	27	66
Chocolate bars	6	16	32	49	67
Wine gums	13	23	34	45	63
Fast food (burgers)	--	1	10	37	72
Deodorant	--	3	19	43	60

Contact with friends is frequent: 95% visit friends 1-3 times a week, with the frequency of being visited by friends also high. 60% do sports activities, and when asked how they would prefer to use an extra hour available, the most frequent answer was to spend it with friends.

All in all, it is evident that diffusion processes occur among children and teenagers. This is the case for entirely new products on the market as well as for exciting products that at one point in time will be new to the child as it matures. In this process, mass media naturally plays an important role, but an often overlooked factor in this diffusion process among children is the role of opinion leaders and innovators. In the following, we shall attempt to gain more insight into their role.

Table 2:7. Children's own shopping

Visiting frequency (%)	8-10 yrs.	11-12 yrs.	13-15 yrs.	16-18 yrs.
Matas *(drugstore)* Weekly	1	8	14	16
Monthly/half-yearly	33	46	52	59
H&M *(fashion)* Weekly	1	7	13	16
Monthly/half-yearly	44	43	36	30
Vero Moda *(fashion)* Weekly	1	4	14	15
Monthly/half-yearly	5	16	30	34
McDonald's Weekly	1	4	8	11
Monthly/half-yearly	68	65	68	70

Innovators and opinion leaders

In the classical Diffusion of Innovation literature, innovators are simply those who adopt first. In empirical studies, one may identify them by observing when they adopt or by asking them questions about this. The latter may be done with the use of specific questions about when a particular innovation was first adopted or in a more generalized way by asking questions about whether the individual sees himself or herself as one who adopts products in general or in specific areas earlier than others (Kapferer and Gilles, 1980; Rogers 1995).

From such studies, we learn that innovators are more in contact with the world outside the social group to which he belongs, they use more mass media, they generally have a higher income and a higher social status, and they are more highly educated (though exceptions occur) (Rogers, 1995).

Opinion leaders, in contrast, are those in the social group to whom people tend to go for advice on new products, new ideas, etc. (Kazt and Lazarsfeld, 1964, 1955). Again, one may establish opinion leadership by studying social interaction in the group and identify the individuals who most people ask for advice in general or in specific areas, or one may try to identify opinion leaders by having people answer questions about how they see themselves in terms of giving advice, influencing others, etc. There tends to be good but not perfect agreement between opinion leaderships identified in the two different ways.

A major research issue in the study of innovators and opinion leaders has been whether generalized innovators and generalized opinion leaders exist, i.e. whether it tends to be the same people who innovate first and are asked for advice in most or all areas (Wärneryd, 1965; Silk 1966; Summers and King, 1969). The findings here are quite unanimous. The existence of a generalized innovator or opinion leader has mostly been disconfirmed. Rather, some people tend to be opinion leaders in some areas but not in others. Nevertheless, there is a tendency towards overlapping opinion leadership, in the sense that people who act as opinion leaders in a particular area, for example stereo equipment, are also more likely to do so in another related area, for example CD players. The same observation is also made about innovators (Robertson and Myers, 1969). On the whole, the more different the product areas studied, the less overlap of innovators there is among them.

A second major issue in the study of innovation has been whether innovators are also opinion leaders or whether the two roles are played largely by different individuals. Here, most studies have shown that innovators are of a different breed than opinion leaders. Although overlap may occur, innovators are less closely affiliated with the social network, they have stronger connections outside the group, they may be more resourceful (intelligence, income, education), and they are more willing to take risks. Opinion leaders, in contrast, are not the very first adopters, but they play an important role among early adopters and in the early majority (Rogers and Shoemaker, 1971).

In the existing literature, two views have been put forward and argued for by different researchers. The traditional view held by (Rogers, 1962) and many other researchers is that the early adopters rarely play an important role as opinion leaders in the social network. Much evidence has been published supporting this view. However, other scholars have argued that rather than talking about opinion leaders and innovators as separate entities, one should look at transmitters as proposed by (Fletcher, 2004). These transmitters are characterized by often being asked advice in a particular area, but they themselves also frequently seek advice from others, i.e. they are those who most frequently act as information transmitters in both directions. In turn, these transmitters also tend to be early adopters of products for which they are transmitters. An early formulation of this point of view was presented by (Cerha, 1967), who talked about people who more or less frequently engage in personal communication. Those who often ask questions are also those who are often asked questions by others. In his terminology, people interested in a particular area tend to be those often exchanging information in the area, and again they tend to have a higher probability of being innovators in that area. In this connection, interesting recent findings are available.

Figure 2:3. Which 3 of the following would make you feel more comfortable about taking out a product or service with a company?

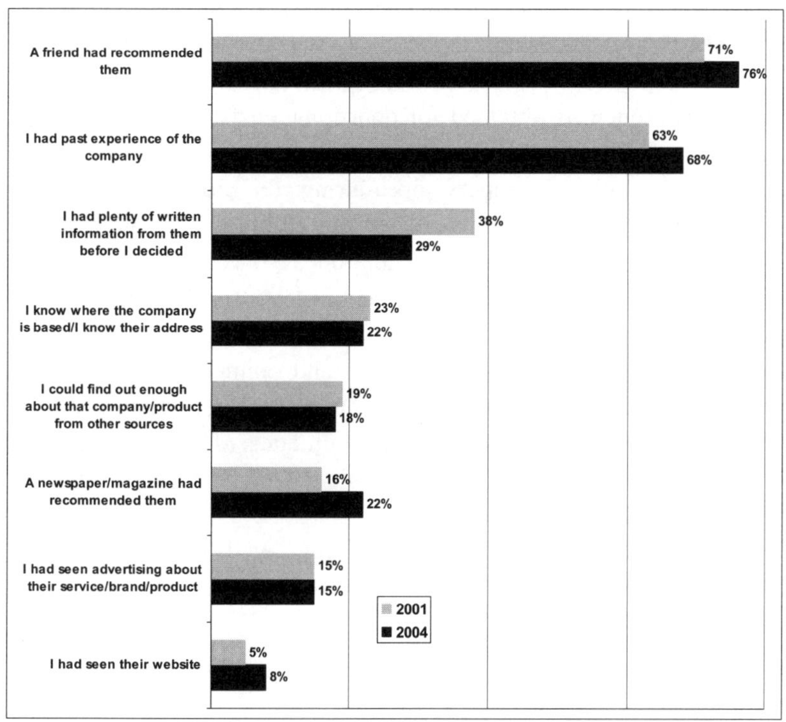

Source: BMRB Omnibus Survey / Royal Mail 2001 / MEC Medialab 2004 (Fletcher, 2004).

A study by The Royal Mail in 2001 was repeated in 2004 by Media Lab in London (Fletcher, 2004). Here, a random sample of respondents was asked what would make them feel most comfortable about taking a product or service by a company. The dominant role of personal information (and personal experiences) is evident. It is remarkable also that among information sources the relative importance of personal recommendation seems to have increased in the time period studied.

In the following, we shall examine these basic issues about opinion leadership and innovativeness among children.

Opinion leadership and innovators among children

The findings to be reported here are based upon a study conducted in 2003 covering a wide range of topics related to children's media use, interest, activities and consumer behaviour.

The data collection method used was questionnaires to be completed at home. This methodology is the same as the one used in the study from which year-2000 data has been reported in the preceding pages. Parental consent was obtained for questionnaires to younger children (12 years or less). In connection with the younger children, the parents accepted the role as supervisors during the completion of the questionnaire. The questionnaires for the children were prepared in three different versions to suit the age groups 5-7 years, 8-12 years and 13-18 years. The survey aimed at having 125 respondents per age group. A reward was offered for the completion of the questionnaire. The critical questions about innovation and opinion leadership were put to the two older age groups. In the present reporting, only the group 8-12 years is included, since most products of concern here tend to be adopted in this age interval (Table 2:1). The pattern found for teenagers will be reported separately.

In total, 822 interviews with children aged 8-12 years were conducted, equally distributed according to sex, age and geographical region in Denmark.

Table 2:8. Early adoption in 8 product categories

	I get new types of clothes … my friends	I get sports equipment … my friends	I get a DVD player … my friends	I get a mobile phone … my friends	I get a MMS mobile phone … my friends	I get a camera mobile phone … my friends	I get computer games … my friends	I hear about text message services … my friends
	Valid percent							
Much earlier than	1.8	1.9	6.7	7.9	1.6	0.6	7.7	1.7
Before	14.7	15.5	14.8	12.9	4.3	1.3	18.0	8.2
Simultaneously with or later than	77.8	70.3	48.7	50.7	40.6	39.0	63.4	53.8
Unanswered	5.7	12.3	29.8	28.5	53.5	59.1	10.9	36.3
Total	100	100	100	100	100	100	100	100

Specific questions were asked about opinion leadership and innovativeness. First, children were asked if they got different products earlier than their friends. The product categories for which questions were asked appear in Table 2:8. Data from a similar question about whether one helps friends and others with the eight product areas selected appear in Table 2:9.

Here, it appears that 2-25% claim to get the different products much before or before friends. An operational measure of innovativeness in particular product areas in the present study could be to consider those answering much before or before as innovators in the area.

Table 2:9. Advising others regarding 8 product areas

	I help with							
	Clothes	Sports equipment	DVD-player	Mobile phone	MMS mobile phone	Mobile camera phone	Computer games	SMS-services
	Valid percent							
None	31.1	43.3	49.9	45.0	69.8	73.1	23.5	54.0
Friends	29.0	33.7	11.7	21.9	13.0	10.9	48.1	20.1
Siblings	16.5	8.5	13.1	5.0	3.6	2.9	18.5	5.2
Parents	19.7	9.5	18.9	22.1	7.9	6.7	6.9	15.7
Others	3.7	5.0	6.5	6.0	5.6	6.3	3.0	5.0
Total	100	100	100	100	100	100	100	100

In Table 2:9, it appears that the extent to which children are advisers to others varies dramatically from 76.5% (computer games) to 26.9% (mobile camera phones). Their role as opinion leaders accrue first and foremost in their giving advice to friends. In the same manner, those indicating that they give advice to friends regarding the eight product categories are designated as opinion leaders in the particular categories.

Next, a count is made in how many areas each respondent is classified as either opinion leader or as innovator. With these data, it is decided that respondents being innovators in three or more product areas are considered to be generalized innovators, and individuals giving advice regarding three or more product categories are considered to be generalized opinion leaders. This makes it possible to study the extent to which generalized opinion leaders are also generalized innovators. By and large, this does not tend to be the case.

*Table 2:10. Innovators * Opinion Leaders*

			Opnion Leaders		
			0-2 areas	3 or more areas	Total
Innovators	0-2 areas	Count	534	176	710
			91.0%	74.9%	86.4%
	3 or more areas	Count	53	59	112
			9.0%	25.1%	13.6%
Total		Count	587	235	822
			100.0%	100.0%	100.0%

From Table 2:10, it appears that out of 235 opinion leaders, only 59 are also innovators. Had data been randomly distributed in the four cells in Table 2:10, we would have expected a total of 32 respondents to fall into the category of both innovator and opinion leader. Thus, we find significantly more than 59, whereas half of those classified as innovators also act as opinion leaders, or reversely, two-thirds of the opinion leaders are not found among innovators. However, the degree of overlap is higher than found in most studies of opinion leadership (Rogers, 1995), but certainly not to a degree where we can argue that being an opinion leader also means being an innovator. According to Rogers' (1962) theory, innovators are seen as the 2.5% who get the new products before others. This may restrict our definition of innovators to those having got the product much earlier than others. In our data (Table 2:10), the innovators make up around 13% of all respondents. To comply with the more strict definition by Rogers, we may limit our definition of innovators to only those having got the product much earlier than others. When this is done, we get a total of 28 respondents being both innovators and opinion leaders, in comparison with 10, which would have been expected by change suggesting that with this more narrow definition of opinion leadership we find important overlap between opinion leadership and innovators.

When we compute the overlap within specific areas, we find the same extent of overlap between opinion leaders and innovators.
Having found that opinion leaders and innovators are somewhat different species, we may look at each of the categories separately. Let us first turn to the innovators.

Overlap among innovators

One way of getting an impression of the extent to which children who are innovators in one area are also innovators in other areas is to conduct a factor analysis based upon the raw data matrixes in Table 2:9. When this is done, it is found that a two-factor solution explains 52% of the total variance in the data. The solution is shown in Table 2:11 in terms of the rotated component matrix. Here, each of the figures reflects the correlation between the answers to the particular question and the so far unnamed factor in the column. The first factor combines high scores on being early on all the electronic devices and activities, whereas computer games groups together with new clothes and sports equipment. In the first factor, the four largest loadings all relate to mobile products. In the last factor, the two most important scores relate to clothing. In between lie the DVD players related to mobile phones and the computer games related to clothing products. Both have much smaller associating with the respective factors and they load quite high on the opposite factor. We may view the first factor as one grouping of innovators on mobile phones with some overlap to DVD players. The second factor we may see as one grouping of clothing with some overlap with games.

Table 2:11. Factor analysis on Innovators

	Component	
	1	2
I get MMS Mobile Phone from my friends	.852	- .038
I get Mobile Camera from my friends	.782	.009
I hear about SMS-Services from my friends	.639	.397
I get Mobile Phone from my friends	.628	.342
I get DVD-Player from my friends	.490	.193
I get new types of clothes from my friends	.077	.783
I get Sports Equipment from my friends	.061	.773
I get Computer Games from my friends	.186	.455

Extraction Method: Principal Component Analysis.
Rotation Method: Varimax with Kaiser Normalization.
Rotation converged in 3 iterations.

Overlap among opinion leadership

A similar analysis can be carried out on the data about opinion leadership. Here the two-factor analysis is shown in Table 2:12. With

62% of the variance in the data explained, it shows a picture much like the one we found in connection with innovators. The two factors only differ from the solution regarding innovativeness, in the sense that computer games have now moved from the second to the first factor, giving us one clear group of 'technically oriented opinion leaders' and another group of 'dress-oriented opinion leaders'. However, it should be noted that here, as in the innovator analysis, DVD and computer games relate almost as closely to the clothing opinion leader factor as they do to the technically oriented opinion leader group.

From where do children get information about new products?

In the study, it was asked for each of the eight product categories from where the child first gets information. Results are reported in Table 2:13. Here, it can be seen that the dominant source is personal information (class mates, friends, siblings and parents) with a total of 44%. This again is distributed with 26.2% on friends and schoolmates and 17.8% on family. The second largest source is television, the third is advertising. Other media play a minor role and it is remarkable that the interactive media (Internet and mobile phones) are of quite limited importance. Only 5.8% mention the Internet as an information source regarding new products. It is worth emphasizing that in a time where attention is heavily directed towards the influence of new media on children's behaviour, the traditional personal and mass media still dominate. It is not clear exactly what the 20% who claim they get information from advertising first are talking about. Most of the product areas examined are not heavily advertised on television. Brochures and other print information must play an important role.

It is interesting to look at innovators and opinion leaders' use of information sources also. Here, we find that opinion leaders tend to rely more heavily on personal communication, and it is particularly communication from friends and schoolmates that is important. In contrast, innovators rely less upon personal communication.

Furthermore, for both opinion leaders and innovators, interactive media play a larger role than they do for the children who do not act as opinion leaders or innovators. Advertising and other media are slightly more used among innovators than others and less among opinion leaders. The overall pattern confirms the picture of opinion leaders and innovators as depicted in general studies of diffusion of innovation.

Innovators tend to rely more upon information sources outside the group (Internet, other media and advertising), whereas the opinion leaders tend to rely more upon information from the closer social network, first and foremost friends and school mates.

There are remarkable differences in the information sources used across the different product categories. Friends and schoolmates play the greatest role for clothing, computer games and sports shoes. In all other product areas, they are less important, and particularly so among innovators.

Table 2:12. Use of Different Information Sources for Opinion Leaders, Innovators and Other among Children aged 8 – 12

	Opinion Leaders	Innovators	Total / All	
	%	%	N	%
Internet	7.7	6.7	253	4.9
Television	22.0	19.5	1265	24.4
Class mates	13.2	12.7	668	12.9
Friends	16.8	11.9	692	13.3
Siblings	6.8	8.3	417	8.0
Parents	8.2	11.2	504	9.7
Radio	0.6	0.4	25	0.5
Newspapers and magazines	5.0	6.7	263	5.1
Advertisements	18.5	21.5	1056	20.4
Mobile phone/SMS	1.1	1.1	45	0.9
Total	100	100	5188	100

Family, particularly parents, play a dominant role for clothing (31% claim they first learn about new clothing from their parents), but also sportswear and mobile phones are heavily influenced by family.

Television plays a dominant role for mobile phones, MMS and mobile cameras.

Advertising plays the most important role for DVD, MMS and mobile cameras, and to a much larger extent so among innovators. For instance, for mobile cameras, 42% claim to get the first information from advertising. Since neither of these product areas are heavily advertised on television, it most be print advertising of various kinds that dominates.

The use of the Internet shows an interesting pattern. It is almost unused in connection with clothing and sports shoes and most heavily regarding MMS and computer games. For all non-clothing categories, innovators tend to rely significantly more upon the Internet than the followers. For opinion leaders, the pattern is pretty much the same. For opinion leaders, the Internet is quite unimportant for clothing and sports equipment, but is quite frequently used in connection with mobile phones, MMS, mobile cameras, computer games and SMS services. With regard to television, its role is less important for clothing and sports shoes, but more important for mobile phones and related products. Mobile phones and advertising on television may account for this. For opinion leaders, personal influence from friends and classmates is extremely important for clothing and sports equipment. When it comes to electronic products and related services, opinion leaders tend to be less influenced by friends and class mates.

Conclusion and further research questions

Opinion leaders and innovators among children are not the same, although the degree of overlap is somewhat greater than in most general studies of opinion leadership and innovativeness. To some extent, one may say that innovators also tend to be opinion leaders, whereas the opposite is much less evident. On the whole, the pattern known in connection with diffusion of innovation can more or less precisely be identified in the way in which children and teenagers adopt new products and products that are new to the maturing child. Particularly, we find that in the adoption process personal communication plays a dominant role, in the sense that this source of information is more relied upon than any other single information source, followed by television and advertising. An interesting research issue is how children combine and evaluate the personal communication on the one hand and television and advertising on the other.

It is remarkable that among the 8-12 years mobile phones and SMS messages play an almost non-existing role in the communication of information about the kind of new products studied here. One might speculate that some of the personal information rated so important may actually imply some use of mobile phones; a point of view which cannot be confirmed with the present data, but which further research will have to reveal. Similar analyses of the 13-18-year-olds may show a different pattern.

As in the general theory of innovation, the innovators tend to rely more heavily on sources external to the daily social group and here the Internet plays a role. However, personal influence is still more important and more so from family than from friends and schoolmates. Television and advertising together play a very important role in dismissing information about new products. More than 20% of the respondents claim that each one of these categories provides them with new information about products. It is not clear from the way that the questions have been asked in the survey how respondents distinguish advertising from television and other media in general. The important role placed on advertising, however, suggests that print advertising, possibly brochures and the like, may be quite important, since many of the products studied are not all, or only modestly, advertised on television.

References

Bejot, M. and B. Doittau (2004); Advertising to Children in France. *International Journal of Advertising and Marketing to Children, Vol. 5, No. 3*, Apr-Jun, pp. 69-72.

Cerha, J. (1967); *Selective Mass Communication.* Stockholm: P.A. Norstedt och Söner.

Feilitzen, C. v. (2002); Times are Changing and Youth with Them – On Young People's Media Use in Sweden in Hansen et al. (ed.), *Children – Consumption, Advertising and Media.* Copenhagen: CBS Press.

Fletcher, D. (2004); *Where's Debbie?* ASI, Barcelona.

Geraci, J.C. and J. Nagy (2004); The Challenge of Advertising to Children. *International Journal of Advertising and Marketing to Children, Vol. 5, No. 2*, Jan-Mar, pp. 8-12.

Hansen, F. et al. (2002a); Danish Children's Upbringing as Consumers in Hansen et al. (ed.), *Children – Consumption, Advertising and Media.* Copenhagen: CBS Press.

Hansen, F. et al. (2002b); *Børns opvækst som forbrugere*. Copenhagen: Samfundslitteratur.

Hansen, F. (1972); *Consumer Choice Behavior – a cognitive theory*. New York.

Howard, J.A. and J.N. Sheth (1969); *A Theory of Buyer Behaviour*. New York: John Wiley and Sons.

Kapferer, J.N. and G. Laurent (1984); *Marketing Analysis on the Basis of the Consumer's Degree of Involvement*. ESOMAR Congress, pp. 223-45.

Kapferer, J.N. and L. Gilles (1980); *Are Early Triers Innovators?* ESOMAR Congress September, 99. pp. 399-415.

Karet, N. (2004); Understanding Children's Responses to TV. *International Journal of Advertising and Marketing to Children, Vol. 5, No. 2,* Jan-Mar, pp. 51-60.

Katz, E., and P.F. Lazarsfeld (1964) (1955); *Personal Influence*. New York: The Free Press.

Nicosia, F.M., (1966); *Consumer Decision Process*. New Jersey: Englewood Cliffs, Prentice-Hall.

Randrup, L. and Lac, K.T. (2000); *Presentation of a Danish Qualitative Study concerning Children*. Copenhagen Business School: Forum for Advertising Research.

Robertson, T.R. and J.G. Myers (1969); Personality Correlates of Opinion Leadership and Innovative Buying Behaviour, *Journal of Marketing Research, Vol. 6*, pp. 164-68.

Rogers, E.M. (1962, 1995); *Diffusion of Innovations*. New York: The Free Press.

Rogers, E.M. (1976); New Product Adoption and Diffusion, *Journal of Consumer Research, Vol. 2, No. 4*, March, pp. 290-302.

Rogers, E.M. (1981); Diffusion of Innovation: An Overview, in Edward B. Roberts et al. (eds), *Biomedical Innovation*. Cambridge. M.I.T. Press-.

Rogers, E.M. and F.F. Shoemaker (1971); *Communication of Innovations*. New York. The Free Press, Macmillan.

Silk, A.J. (1966); Overlap Among Self-Designated Opinion Leaders, *Journal of Marketing Research, Vol. 3*, pp. 255-60.

Summers, J.O. and C.W. King (1969); *Interpersonal Communications and New Product Attitude*. Paper presented at the Fall Conference of the American Marketing Association in Cincinnati, Ohio.

Tufte, B. (2003); *Girls in the New Media Landscape*. Nordicom Review.

Wärneryd, B. (1965); *Innovation, inflydelse og information*. Stockholm: Almquist och Wicksell.

3

Children, TV Advertising and the Law – Internal and External Perspectives

LENA OLSEN

The problem

Children, i.e. persons below the age of legal capacity in accordance with the national rules[1], which in Sweden is 18 years, are important actors in the market. According to one Swedish report, Swedish teenagers have considerable amounts of money at their disposal. Specifically, children between 13 and 17 have around 4,785 million SEK per year of pocket money and other income at their disposal (Samuel, 2003: p. 22)[2]. Much of this goes into savings, but the rest is spent on products such as clothes and hygiene, media, junk food, for example hamburgers and sweets, transport, telephones, beer and tobacco (Samuel: p. 23ff). Also younger children are a bigger consumer group than one would expect. According to another Swedish report, these age groups have 706 million SEK in pocket money at their disposal, which is obviously much lower than for older children but still impressive (Samuel, 2001: p. 13)[3]. Even if the spending freedom is probably more restricted by the parents (Johansson: p.

---

[1] UN Convention of the Rights of the Child, Article 1. In the following, persons below 18 years will most often be referred to as children.

[2] The amounts of yearly income stated in the report are here multiplied with 85,000 persons. Each generation amounts to between 90,000 and 120,000 persons. Some are handicapped and some do not even get any money. The figure 85,000 has thus been chosen with the purpose not to exaggerate. See also Hansen, F., Halling, J. and Nielsen, J.C.(2004), The economic power of children, in Olsen, L. (ed), *Barns makt*, p. 84f. for information regarding the Danish situation.

[3] Also here, the amounts are multiplied with 85,000 persons, cf. footnote 2.

11ff)[4], and even if a considerable proportion goes into savings (Samuel, 2001: p. 21), there still ought to be a considerable amount to spend on products such as toys, "foods" like sweets and fast food, media and, increasingly, clothes and presents (Ibid). It thus appears that children are an important consumer group of the products they buy. Besides the private consumption of children, children play an important role in connection with the consumption of the family as a whole[5], and they have also an impressive knowledge of trademarks (Hansen, Halling and Nielsen, 2004: p. 87ff). All this could explain why children have increasingly become an important target for advertising.

Despite the huge economic importance of children, the legislator has taken action only to a limited extent. The general Swedish legislation relating to marketing is the Marketing Act (1995:450). However, there are no specific legal rules within this Act which expressly relate to children[6]. Instead, important rules are found in the *traveaux preparatoire* and case law. Thus, particular consideration should be given to the fact that advertising directed towards children could be misleading (Prop. 1970:57, p. 69). It is also forbidden to target direct advertising at children below the age of 16, as this could induce them to try to persuade parents or other guardians to buy the advertised product (MD 1996:26) (See also Svensson, Stenlund, Brink and Ström (2002) p. 506). Besides these general rules, there are in particular a few rules concerning children and TV advertising in the Radio and TV Act (1996:844). There is no specific legislation at all governing advertising in the new media[7].

Thus, it appears that the legal problems which arise in connection with children and advertising have not been given overall consideration by the legislator, even though there are a number of legal rules or other kinds of rules laid down by, for example, the Consumer Ombudsman or the International Chamber of Commerce (ICC) that deal with the particular difficulties for children. Where such particular problems are not specifically addressed, children are regarded as members of the general public. This hidden position could create difficulties in the overall evaluation of the legal position of children.

---

[4] Cf. (Johansson, B.; *Barn som aktörer i konsumtionssamhället*, p.11ff.)

[5] In relation to electronic products, see Hansen, Halling and Nielsen (footnote 2) p. 85-86.

[6] The same appears to be the case in the Danish Marketing Act.

[7] However, the Nordic Consumer Ombudsmen have issued guidelines for this field as well as the International Chamber of Commerce (ICC).

Children are discussed in a scholarly manner from a number of angles. One point of particular interest for the articles in this book is the distinction between the child as a vulnerable "social becoming" and the child as a competent "social being". In this article, the latter aspect, i.e. the extent to which children are able to participate in different kinds of "legal" processes that concern them, is of particular importance. This question could also be put in terms of power, and therefore a research model has been developed on the basis of political science and law in order to evaluate the legal system.

However, when presenting and discussing the law, it is necessary to be aware of the distinction between the internal and external perspective of the law, and the consequences of this for the possible theory and method.

Thus, in the first part of the chapter, it is necessary to deal with the internal and external approach to law and the consequences of this from a methodological point of view. Then the Swedish legislation is dealt with using an internal perspective focussing on the substantial rules. In the third part of the chapter the field is discussed from an external perspective, the objective being to evaluate the power of the child in relation to children and TV advertising. In order to do this, it is necessary to briefly present a research model, which will then be used in relation to the relevant legislation. Finally, some conclusions are drawn.

The internal and external perspective of the law

As has been mentioned, the law could be discussed in two fundamentally different ways (Olsen, 2004: p. 108ff). It could be discussed from an internal perspective. In this respect, the relevant question to ask is: what is the applicable law? In other words, what rules could possibly be applied by a court or a particular state authority[8]. Beside judges, prosecutors, legal counsellors, etc., this knowledge is also important for the ordinary citizen. It could also be of interest for legislator, as it is often important to decide first what the law is in order to be able to see the problems with it and then start the discussion about possible and necessary changes[9].

---

[8] For the internal perspective and the consequences of it for the research cf. (Olsen, 2004: pp. 111-122).

[9] For a discussion of the needs of different receivers of legal research cf. (Olsen, 2004: pp. 132-140 with references).

The other fundamental way to regard the law is to use an external perspective (Olsen, 2004: p. 109). In such a case, the relevant question is not to know what the law is for its proper application, but rather to discuss other problems, such as how the courts actually reach their decisions; what similarities and differences are there between the law in one country and the law in another country, or what influences from other sciences could be used directly in connection with the legal rules (Olsen, 2004: pp. 122-132).

The distinction between an internal and external perspective is partly important from a methodological point of view. If you want to know the applicable law, i.e. apply the internal perspective, it is important to find the most authoritative sources, which differ slightly between different countries and legal cultures. In the Nordic countries, the legislated acts are the most important, and to some extent are complemented through the *traveaux preparatoire* by the government. Occasionally, the reports are also made within the parliamentary handling. Regulations are also binding. However, not all rules are to be found in legislation or regulations. Many rules are also found in the case law, i.e. cases from the highest courts, and, occasionally, remarks in the legal literature may be of importance.

One might believe that legislation is binding. This is, however, not always the case. It depends partly on the relevant legal area and the wording of the legal text. Criminal law is, of course, binding and the administrative law is binding to a large extent. However, the legislation could also draw attention to other forms of material, which could assume a more important role. In relation to marketing, the Marketing Act refers to good commercial practices, and very important sources as to the content of such good practices in Sweden are guidelines and recommendations from the Consumer Ombudsman and the ICC's Codes and Guidelines, in particular the ICC Code of Advertising Practices. However, it is the court that ultimately decides whether the code or guideline constitutes a good commercial practice.

Research using an external approach is less restricted in relation to the choice of material and how it is handled. The choice depends, as always, on what one wants to achieve. Thus, theories or methods from other sciences could be used, although such a study could never amount to a description of the applicable law. Thus, if the purpose of the research project is to come as close as possible to the applicable law, it is naturally important to focus as much as possible on the most authoritative material. The same is often the case if the purpose is rather to achieve some sort of evaluation of the law. However, systematisations or evaluations, etc. could also be based on a more limited range of rules.

The applicable Swedish law concerning children and TV advertising

The Radio and TV Act (1996:844) (RTVA) and children

The Radio and TV Act implements the TV Without Frontiers Directives (89/552/EEG and 97/36/EG), even if this is not the only task to be performed in connection with the Act. For the purposes of this article, the most interesting provisions are found in Chapter 7, where there are a number of rules of importance in relation to children and advertising, i.e. Sections 4 and 7b. These rules go beyond the rules in the directive, which are applicable when TV advertising appears on TV from other EU Member States. Thus, the Swedish rules are applicable in relation to national TV or broadcasting to the EEA area, for example when the broadcaster is situated in Sweden, RTVA 1:2.

Sweden has a history of caution in connection with TV advertising and children. The legislator refers in this connection to the particular penetrating power of TV as a medium especially among children, the difficulty for younger children to distinguish between advertising and ordinary television programmes, and their difficulty to realize that the purpose of advertising is partly to bring about sales contracts (Prop. 1990/91:149, p. 121). To allow TV advertising is thus regarded to be contrary to the interests of children (Prop. 1990/91:149, p. 121).

These views have led to several rules particularly dealing with children and advertising. The rules can broadly be divided into three groups: rules prohibiting advertising targeted at children below the age of 12 years, rules dealing with the content of the advertising, and rules dealing with the placing of the advertising.

The particular rules concerning children and advertising

The prohibition of advertising:
The most well-known rule is found in RTVA 7:4(1), according to which TV advertising that attracts the attention of children below the age of 12 is prohibited. The purpose of the rule was from the beginning to protect younger children, i.e. those who had not yet reached puberty. To clarify this, the legislator chose the age of 12 years (Prop.

1990/91:149, p. 121). The wording "attracts the attention" is slightly unclear. The prohibition specifically covers advertising only directed towards children below the age of 12 years. However, it does not cover advertising directed towards children below the age of 12 **and** persons above that age, despite the fact the advertising may attract the attention of younger children (Prop. 1990/91:149, p. 123; MD 2001:5). A better wording would thus have been that the advertising is "directed towards" (Prop. 1990/91:149, p. 123).

There are three points of particular importance in connection with the assessment: firstly, the offered goods or service; secondly, the content and design of the advertising; and thirdly, the relevant context ((Prop. 1990/91:149, p. 122). All these aspects must point to the conclusion that the advertising is directed towards children below the age of 12. The fact that the advertising concerns a toy or something that is primarily of interest for children is not enough. Consequently, the TV advertising of the Disney movie "Cinderella" was not regarded as attracting the attention of children, on the grounds that it was not elaborated in such a way and it was not broadcast during such a time when young children constitute an important group of the viewers (MD 2001:5).

The content of advertising:
According to RTVA 7:4(2), there may not in TV advertising appear persons or characters which play an important part in programmes that are primarily directed towards children below the age of 12 years. This means that not only are Swedish figures prohibited but also characters or persons from other countries as long as the programmes are received in Sweden (Prop. 1990/91:149 p. 123).

Other rules concerning the content of advertising directed towards children and young people are found in connection with the Marketing Act, which partly state that advertising may not be misleading. According to the *traveaux preparatoire*, the requirements in this regard are more stringent when children or young people are involved (Prop. 1970:69 which is still the rule).

The placing of the advertising:
There are a number of rules that deal with the placing of advertising for the purpose of protecting children. Firstly, programmes attracting the attention of children below the age of 12 may not be interrupted by advertising, RTVA 7:7b(1). Secondly, advertising in general may not be broadcast immediately before or after a children's programme or as

part of such a programme, irrespective of at whom it is directed (RTVA 7:7b (3)). The purpose of this rule is to stop advertising of considerable interest for children, including advertising for such products as cereals and chocolate (Prop. 1995/96:160, p. 116). Thirdly, a more problematic rule is found in RTVA 6:2, which is an implementation of the TV directive. According to this rule, a programme, which contains presentations of realistic violence or pornography may not be broadcast at such a time or in such a way as to create a substantial risk for children to see it.[10] If the RTVA does not impose any minimum requirements as to violence and pornography, one could again turn to the Marketing Act and its reference to good marketing standards, which are also laid down in the ICC Code of Advertising Practices 1997. According to Article 2, advertisements should not contain statements or visual presentations, which offend prevailing standards of decency, and according to Article 4.3, advertisements should not appear to condone or incite violence, nor to encourage unlawful or reprehensible behaviour. Advertising which contravenes these provisions should generally not be covered by the Marketing Act, as it involves freedom of speech issues[11]. Preferably, these contraventions may be reported to the Council on Market Ethics (MER), which, however, could only react with a statement.

Effects of the rules for children below and above 12 years

The abovementioned rules are not easy to perceive. It may therefore be sensible to try to describe the effects of the rules for children of different ages.

First, the thought is that children below the age of 12 should not be subjected to any advertising at all which is directed towards them. Secondly, they should only be confronted with well-known characters and persons in the children's programmes, and not in advertising directed towards older children and adults. This rule is essential, as the question of whether advertising is directed towards children below the age of 12 is judged through the deliberation of three aspects: the

---

[10] Here, one important question arises regarding whether advertising is considered to constitute a 'programme'. However, the wording of RTVA 6:3 and 6:4 indicate that such is the case, as they say that 'programmes, that is not advertising'.

[11] However, cf (MD 1996:7).

product or service, the content and design of the advertisement, and the relevant context. Thus, advertising may not necessarily be directed towards younger children simply because important characters or persons from children's programmes appear in the advertising. At the same time, such figures are regarded as something that strongly attracts the interest of children. Thirdly, children below the age of 12 years should not be subjected to any advertising at all immediately before, during or after children's programmes.

Children above the age of 12 years are also to some extent protected through the abovementioned rules. Thus, if they watch TV4, which is financed through advertising, they should not come into contact with advertising directed towards children below the age of 12 years. This could be good especially for those children close to 12 years of age or maturity. Furthermore, if they look at children's programmes, they will not meet advertising immediately before, during or after the programme. If they look at other programmes, they do not have to see familiar figures from the children's programmes. This could probably be of value for the younger teenagers. In all other respects they are regarded as adults, which means the Swedish Marketing Act is applicable with its rules concerning misleading advertising.

To the extent that advertising may be regarded as a programme, it may not contain too much violence or pornography during normal viewing hours. This rule probably protects younger more than older children.

An external view of the relevant legislation – the power of children to act

Introduction

In the text above, the rules to be applied, i.e. the internal perspective, have been described. However, such a perspective does not permit any conclusions as to the power of the child in different respects. To reach such conclusions, it is important to analyse the relevant legislation with other tools. I have chosen to do it using a particular model, based on different aspects of power found particularly in political but also social sciences, and 'translated' to the legal 'reality'.

The model[12]

This part of the chapter is based on (Olsen, 2004: p. 103 ff.). In order to analyse and assess the content of the rules and their importance for the position of the individual child, a particular analysis is needed of what power the child has over itself and its everyday life. The concept of power within other sciences than law is a possible point of departure and I have chosen to use the principal discussion of it by (Pettersson, 1987: pp. 7ff).

One fundamental issue in connection with power is the meaning of the concept. The lexical meaning of the word includes the idea of competence to do things, as well as the capacity to exert an influence on other persons (Pettersson 1987: p. 9). Both these meanings are of interest from a legal perspective, as both competence and relation are legally important. It is clear that the capacity of children is limited in both these respects. The fact that children have neither competence nor capacity must thus be considered as well.

A closely related matter is the problem of whether an actual use of power is necessary for the discussion (Pettersson, 1987: p. 13). Such could not be the case in relation to a study of legal rules, as these generally provide possibilities, both in a positive and negative sense. The power provided for in legal rules is thus latent, until the prerequisites stated in the rule are fulfilled. Then the power is actually existent.

The fact that someone could influence someone or something through the causality between an act and its effect is regarded as one type of power (Pettersson, 1987: p. 13f). Examples of this that are important within the law are provisions in relation to crime and damages. Even in other situations the phenomenon could be considered in connection with the law. Not all children suffer terrible experiences when their parents divorce. However, it is obvious that life is unfair and the law adapts to this fact.

The view of power as a relationship between two or more actors is, as mentioned above, important within law. Thus, comprehensive groups of rules deal with this particular problem, such as private law, etc. In these cases, it is important to note which person could act and towards whom. It is also important, in particular in relation to children, to note to what extent the child could take action by itself or if the support by, for example, parents is necessary or recommendable. Thus,

---

[12] This part of the article is based on Olsen, L. (2004); Barns makt som konsumenter" in Olsen, L. (ed.) *Barns makt,* p. 103ff.

it is necessary to ascertain the subject of the power, the prerequisites for the competence of the subject, and towards whom the power is used, i.e. the personal object. Persons of particular importance here are parents, school staff, traders, etc. As parents could be the subject of power as well as the personal object, it is important to be clear about the difference. In the following discussion, the possibilities of children to act will be primarily considered.

In relation to the content of the law and the assessment of it, it is also important to consider the general conditions for the power. Here, Pettersson talks about the resources for power ("maktresurser") (Pettersson, 1987: 15). Such a concept is, however, too indistinct for a legal discussion. Instead, all the legal prerequisites for the possible action have to be considered, such as the relevant parties.

As has been mentioned, power could mean to act in a certain way or to exert influence on someone. Thus, what could be done by the child is an important part of the evaluation and also the particular prerequisites for it. However, the problem is that the legislator has not elaborated these aspects in connection with children. Despite this, there are sometimes possibilities for the child to exert influence over other persons, in which case the power could be described as active (Pettersson, 1987: 12). If the power merely could be said to concern the competence of the child, it could be called passive. Finally, it is also important to be able to describe the situation when the legislation does not give the child any possibilities at all to act or to exert influence, which could be called non-power. The part that the child is allowed to play could thus be an active part, a passive part and a non-part (Pettersson, 1987).

As has been seen, a number of different aspects could be of interest in relation to an analysis of the legal power of children. The purpose is to be able to analyse and describe the child's actual possibilities to act and the prerequisites for this, as well as to find out when no such possibilities to act exist. The model could be summarized in the following way. It consists of five closely connected aspects: what could be done (the material object of the power), who could do it (the subject), how to decide the relevant competence and towards whom the power could be directed (the personal object), and finally, an assessment of the part the child could play has to be made[13].

---

[13] Other concepts for these aspects are used in the Swedish article. No difference, however, is intended.

1) *The content of the power – the material object.* The rule could state a number of prerequisites for the child's possibility to act in a broad sense. The prerequisites could deal with such aspects as the context of the relevant action (e.g. the school or the family) or as a thing to do, for instance to conclude some particular sort of contract, sit on the board of a school or vote for children's school representatives, but also to receive information from the social welfare officers.

2) *Who could do it – the subject.* Traditionally, the focus has been directed towards what the child/parents or guardians could do. However, with the new focus on children's participation and empowerment, it is necessary to separate the two. The most important aspect within this new field of research should therefore be what the child could or could not do.

3) *The competence of the child.* The period of childhood ranges from newborns to 18 years. It is clear that a newborn cannot do what a 17-year-old can. Thus, the law must take a stance in the relevant situation as to the appropriate age limit or requirements as to maturity that should be required for the child being able to act. One advantage with the method of referring to different age limits is the foreseeability this creates. One disadvantage is, however, that children mature differently. The reference to the actual maturity of the individual child could be good as it relates to the actual state of affairs, but it could also be difficult to prove and thus lead to a lesser degree of foresee ability. There are also other solutions in between these possibilities. Generally, it is recommendable to differ between when the competence is based on facts possible of external verification (formal competence) and where the individual maturity of the child is of importance (material competence).

4) *Towards whom could the power be directed – the personal object.* The possibilities to act differ depending on the particular person towards whom the child reacts. As the child and its parents/guardians earlier have been intertwined, it has not been regarded as necessary to consider this. As the capacity to act is fairly restricted for children, it is important to differ between the different legal relationships of the child. One set of rules is often applicable for the relationship between the child and its parents/guardians, and another for the relationship towards, for example, the school.

5) *The power of the child as actor.* The points made above could now be evaluated as to the possibilities to act and to influence others. Thus, it is important to differ between cases *when* the child's actions should be considered by the other party, *when* the child may act without the obligation on the other party to take notice of it, and, finally, *when* the child is not allowed to do anything at all. In the first case, the child could be said to have an *active power* in the second it could be said to have a *passive power,* and in the last case the child could be said to play a *non-power.* The active power comes into play when the child may conclude a contract, say yes/no to a certain decision (veto), or assert a certain influence or culture. To provide information that the other party has to consider could also be considered as an active power, as well as being able to force the authorities to provide information. Examples of a passive power could be where a child is allowed to furnish a person with information without that person being obliged to consider it.

The method

As the purpose here is not to identify the applicable law, there is no need to examine all authoritative material that ordinarily is needed for that purpose. The following analysis will therefore be based mainly on the existing legislation or regulations covering the relevant issues. This material will be interpreted in accordance with the lexical meaning of the words.

The relevant legislation as to relevant government authorities

As has been seen, the Swedish rules protecting children particularly below the age of 12 years are of different kinds and involve different government authorities, and it is these that are regulated.

The task of the Consumer Ombudsman is to ensure that TV advertising does not attract the attention of children below the age of 12 (RTVA 7:4 (1) and 9:2 (2)). This authority is also responsible for ensuring that those persons or characters that play an important role in children's programmes do not appear in TV advertising. If this happens, the Consumer Ombudsman may turn to the Market Court on the basis of the Section 4 of the Marketing Act and demand a prohibition of the advertising on the grounds that it contravenes the law, cf. Section 14. Such prohibition is normally combined with a penalty. If the Market Court should issue a prohibition and the broadcaster should contravene it, the Consumer Ombudsman may go to the ordinary courts and either ask for the payment of the penalty or demand a market disruption fee.

The Swedish Broadcasting Commission is responsible for monitoring the placing of the advertising in relation to children's programmes. As has been seen above, children's programmes may not be interrupted by advertisements and there may not be any advertising at all in direct connection with children's programmes. The monitoring is performed post-broadcast (not through censorship).

The Chancellor of Justice is responsible for monitoring that programmes do not contain too much violence or pornography. However, this authority relies on monitoring performed by the Swedish Broadcasting Commission, and where it finds evidence of such content it is required to make a report to the Chancellor of Justice (RTVA 9:2 (4)). To some extent, the Marketing Act could serve as a basis for the Consumer Ombudsman to turn to the Market Court in connection with violence in advertising (MD 1996: 7).

Outside the legal possibilities, the Consumer Ombudsman or even the general public may, as has already been mentioned, turn to the Council on Market Ethics (MER), which is a trader's authority with competence to criticize advertising that contravenes the ICC Code of Advertising Practices (Stadgar för Marknadsetiska Rådet MER, 2004).

Application of the model

The content of the power – the material object:
Not surprisingly, there are no provisions at all which refer to children or children representatives. This does not necessarily mean that the child is renounced of possibilities to act. One possibility to act that hardly needs any legislation is the possibility to report contraventions of the law to the relevant authorities. However, this presupposes that children are aware of the law and concur with it. Thus, it is more likely that children above the age of 12 should manage to report possible contraventions against children below that age. As there is a total ban on TV advertising attracting the attention of children below the age of 12 years, there should be no possibility for children to receive such TV

advertising, except through the choice of an international TV channel, such as TV3 or TV5[14].

Another possibility to act could be to demand damages in accordance with Section 29 of the Marketing Act, which is possible when someone deliberately or through negligence has contravened a prohibition ordered by the court. However, the application of this rule is more complicated. To be able to claim damages, the actual damage has to be a pure property injury. Personal injuries are not covered by the rule, which includes "moral" damages. However, it is hard to see how a child who has been looking at TV advertising could suffer property injury, unless the advertising is misleading, which is not covered by the prohibition of TV advertising addressed to children below the age of 12. Even if a child had gone directly to buy the advertised product, it would be very difficult to say that this purchase has been predominately caused by the relevant advertising. Under all circumstances, the amount of money that children below the age of 12 normally spend on the buying of a certain consumer goods is comparatively low. Thus, it appears that the claiming of damages could hardly be considered an actual power in such a situation. It should also be remembered that moral risks for children such as violence or pornography are not covered by any particular liability to pay damages.

However, personal injuries could be covered by the rules relating to damages in non-contractual situations. Thus, according to Section 2(1) of the Damages Act (1972:207), the person, who deliberately or through negligence adequately causes personal injury to someone else shall pay damages. Generally, it would not be easy to prove that the child has actually seen the relevant advertising and become injured as a result, so a claim for damages is not likely to succeed.

To summarize, children are thus generally limited to reporting contraventions of the law to the relevant authorities, and there are practically no possibilities to claim damages.

Towards whom could the power be directed – the personal object:
A claim for damages could generally be directed towards the trader, who sells the product or offers the service, or towards the broadcaster. It could also be directed towards the advertising agency.

If the trader, broadcaster or advertising agency does not pay, the claim has to be taken to the ordinary courts. Here, the procedural rules

---

[14] Unless the broadcaster contravenes the law.

73

are applicable, and where children are concerned certain rules in the Code of Procedure (RB) apply.

A reported contravention of the TV advertising rules could primarily be made to the Consumer Ombudsman and the Swedish Broadcasting Commission.

Finally, a relationship that is often taken for granted, but is governed by specific rules in the Parental Code, is the one between the child and its parents/guardians, and here it is not certain that the interests of children and parents coincide in all situations. The parents may not want to subscribe to TV3 or TV5 because they contain advertising directed towards children, but the opposite situation could also be possible, i.e. that the parents enjoy all the advertising and the children do not.

Who could do it and how is the child's competence decided:
In relation to the trader, there is no legal limitation for the child itself to claim damages when damaged, as the child is the relevant party, cf. RB 11:1. From a practical point of view, however, few children are able to make such a claim in a reliable way. Furthermore, a claim from a child could hardly be threatening, so generally the guardian is the one who will take care of the financial interests of the child. In the court, this is necessary, cf. RB 11:2 and 20:1. The competence is thus formally decided. A child, i.e. a person below the age of 18 may not go to court with a complaint.

In relation to the Consumer Ombudsman and the Swedish Broadcasting Commission, however, the person who makes the report or the age of this person should hardly be important. The important thing should be the arguments put forward and the way this is done. It should also be remembered that the Consumer Ombudsman, according to the instruction, should particularly support weaker consumer groups (Förordning 1995:868). This means that the competence will be materially decided.

The only legal possibility to receive advertising which attracts the interest of children below the age of 12 years is to subscribe to such channels that contain such TV advertising.

The power of the child as actor:
As has been seen, the possibilities of the child to act are generally limited to making reports to the Consumer Ombudsman and the Swedish Broadcasting Commission. As these reports will not necessarily lead to a reaction, the power could be said to be passive.

In connection with claims for damages, the child could, in principle, make a claim for damages against the trader, broadcaster or advertising agency. The trader is under no obligation to respond to a private claim, so it appears to be a passive power here as well. In the real world, this does not constitute an actual possibility. In relation to the court, the child has no power to act at all.

Conclusions

As has been seen, the Swedish legislator has not realized that children are becoming increasingly more important actors on the consumer market. The legislation is very scattered.

Within the framework of the internal perspective, the most important rule is the total ban on TV advertising. Such a total ban constitutes a risk in relation to the right of information in Article 13 of the UN Convention of the Rights of the Child, and it could be discussed whether the Swedish rule is compatible with the UN Convention.[15] It is not possible to discuss this question here. However, it is important to stress that the Swedish ban on TV advertising is limited in a number of respects.

Firstly, the ban only relates to children below the age of 12 years, i.e. younger children. Secondly, it is applicable only to advertising broadcast on a Swedish channel. Channels emanating from other European countries, even if they broadcast in Swedish, are required to follow EC rules, which do not contain any total ban on TV advertising targeted at younger children. Thirdly, the prohibition only covers TV advertising that solely targets young children. Mixed messages, such as advertising targeted at both young children and adults, are not covered (Olsen, 2002: p. 112). Fourthly, the prerequisite that advertising attracts the attention of children also involves a judgement of three sub-prerequisites: the importance of the offered goods or service, the content and design of the advertising, and the context of the advertising. It is not enough that the advertising, for example, depicts children or concerns toys.

From an external perspective and with the use of a certain model, I have also tried to see what the consequences of the scattered rules are in relation to the possible actions of children themselves. As has been

---

[15] It should be stressed that there is no provision in the UN Convention dealing with commercial exploitation of children that involves advertising or other kinds of marketing.

seen above, there are very few ways for children or their representatives to act if they do not want the TV advertising they receive, and there are practically no possibilities to claim damages regardless of whether they want advertising or not. To enhance the power of children and/or their representatives, it might be an idea to discuss the introduction of punitive damages.

Despite the fact that children's possibilities for legal action from a practical perspective could be seen as a non-power, one should not forget that there are also non-legal ways of taking action. The publicly most important possibility to act is to report contraventions of the law to the Consumer Ombudsman or the Swedish Broadcasting Commission, and this is best done by older children. However, this possibility is not directly provided for in the legislation.

The legal model of scattered prohibitions makes it difficult to assess the position of children, and the legislation in relation to advertising is apparently directed towards the child as a vulnerable "social becoming". However, there are also a few signs that suggest that this is not the only possible way to approach the area. The freedom of information expressed in Article 13 of the UN Convention of the Rights of the Child is the most important example. A wider approach is also possible within legal research, which helps to clarify the position of the child in a wider sense. It might also be necessary with a revision of the law relating to advertising in order to understand the position of the child (and other weak persons) and the arguments of importance.

References

Förordning (1995:868) med instruktion för konsumentverket

Hansen, F.; Halling, J. and J.C. Nielsen (2004); The economic power of children in Olsen, L. (ed.), *Barns makt*. Uppsala: Iustus Förlag AB.

Johansson, B.; *Barn som aktörer i konsumtionssamhället.*
http://www.handelsgu.webhotel.tripnet.sw/files/cfk/general/artikelbarb
rojohansson.pdf

Marknadsdomstolens domar (MD) 2001:5.

Marknadsdomstolens domar (MD) 1999:26.

Marknadsdomstolens domar (MD) 1996:7.

Olsen, L. (2004); Rättsvetenskapliga perspektiv. *Svensk Juristtidning*, p. 106.

Olsen, L. (2004); Barns makt som konsumenter in Olsen, L. (ed.), *Barns makt*. Uppsala: Iustus Förlag AB.

Olsen, L. (2002); Children and Internet Trade in Seipel (ed.), *Law and Information Technology. Swedish views*. Swedish Government Official Reports (SOU): 112.

Pettersson, O. (1987); in O. Pettersson (ed), *Maktbegreppet, Introduktion*. Stockholm: Carlsson.

Proposition 1970:57 med förslag till lag om otillbörlig marknadsföring.

Proposition 1990/91:149 om radio och TV-frågor.

Proposition 1995/96:160 Radio och TV-lag.

Samuel, U. (2003); *Tonåringarna och deras pengar*. Institutet för privatekonomi. Föreningssparbanken och samverkande banker.

Samuel, U. (2001); *Veckopengen IV*. Institutet för privatekonomi. Föreningssparbanken och samverkande banker.

Stadgar for Marknadsetiska Rådet MER (2004). *http://www.marknadsetiskaradet.org*

Svensson, C.A.; Stenlund, A.; Brink, T. and L-E. Ström (2002); *Praktisk marknadsrätt*. Seventh edition. Stockholm: Norstedts Juridik AB.

UN Convention of the Rights of the Child.

4

Young People and Consumption: Commonalities and Differences in the Construction of Identities

ANN PHOENIX

From the start of academic interest in it, consumption was recognised to have important links with identity. While it is an important source of identity for everyone, the 'rise of the teenager' in the 1950s gave a particular focus to youth, identity and consumption. This has been extended down the age range as consumption has become increasingly important to the identities of children in 'middle' childhood who are sometimes referred to as 'tweenagers'. This chapter aims to examine the ways in which consumption is central to young people's identities and social relations. It both draws on the available literature and uses young people's accounts from three research studies to demonstrate some common themes in young people's constructions of consumption and the ways in which social class, gender and 'race' differentiates their consumption.

The first part of the chapter considers the place of consumption in young people's identities in general. The second part of the chapter examines some of the peer group conflicts to do with consumption in which young people engage – as individuals, in groups and in relation to gender, social class and ethnicity. The final part of the chapter considers transactions between young people and their parents in relation to resources for consumption.

The two studies that inform this chapter are the Masculinities study of 11-14 year old London boys' masculine identities (Frosh, Phoenix and Pattman, 2002) and a study (currently being written up) of Consuming Identities: Young people, cultural forms and negotiations in households done by Chris Griffin, Ann Phoenix, Rosaleen Croghan and Janine Hunter. The Economic and Social Research Council funded both the masculinities study and the 'consumption' study. The 'consumption' study was of 12-13-year-old and 17-18-year-old young people in schools in Birmingham, Milton Keynes and Oxford. It focused on the ways in which young people use consumption to construct their identities and to negotiate with their parents for household resources to support their consumption and how social class, ethnicity, 'race', gender and urban or rural location affected these identities and negotiations. The data collected included questionnaires with over 1300 young people, 60 group interviews, 19 individual interviews, 23 interviews on photographs young people had taken with the cameras we had given them and 20 interviews with parents (almost all mothers). The study also included an ethnographic element in which two researchers went shopping with young people, went to clubs and community projects and stayed with them outside a shopping centre.

Consumption and young people's identities

Before the Second World War, young people were not identified as a group on the basis of their appearance, tastes in music, films or clothes. However, as the age of compulsory education rose and young people increasingly needed educational qualifications to secure employment, the transitional period between childhood and adulthood lengthened. At the same time, many young people had more resources available to them – whether they were in employment or education. They received public attention because they had power in the market place that was helping to produce changes in the culture and leisure industries. As a result, young people became a group to be defined by their consumption. This consumption was focused on leisure (rather than work), on peer group identity (rather than family) and on style – with young people displaying creativity in constructing meaning through style. In the 1950s 'youth' increasingly became a focus of media attention and of identification for teenagers on the basis of their consumption (Abrams, 1959).

A further way in which consumption is central to young people's identities concerns their place in the world. Consumption is argued to allow young people to feel that they have a place (through their peer groups) in a rapidly changing world (Miles et al., 1998). It may provide protection against meaninglessness since (as Furby, 1978, suggests) it allows young people some power over their lives and identities. Consumption may thus provide young people with a relatively easy way in which they can symbolically engage in 'identity projects' (attempts to mould identities to move towards a desired identity, Foucault, 1977). It is because it is so important to young people's identities and their place in their peer groups that, while 'youth style' is often seen as trivial by older people, it is of great importance to many young people, even those who may be sceptical about advertising and 'designer' labels.

While consumption practices have important effects on individuals, they can also have wider social impact. For example, in recent years, youth researchers have pointed out that digital technology is transforming the ways in which young people manage their social relations and identities (Langager, 2004). (Rheingold, 2002) coined the term 'swarming' to describe how young people can, for example use SMS technology (texting) to keep in touch with large numbers of people with whom they are in touch (the swarm – which can be global in the virtual 'swarm'), without having to be in one social group. As a result, more effort has to be expended in keeping in touch with members of the swarm, which explains why it is so common for young people who are together to be speaking to, or SMSing (texting), others.

The place of brands in young people's identities

Young people are not cultural dupes or 'fashion victims' (Miles, 2000; Gunter and Furnham, 1998). Indeed, when talking about their style identities, many are adamant that they consider themselves individuals rather than objects of media and advertising manipulation (Widdicombe and Wooffitt, 1995). However, brand name goods are of importance to many young people (as well as some older people). This is because the brands we buy and use can support our ideal identities and show other people the identity and values we want to project. (Sherry, 1998) used the term "brandscapes" to indicate that we live in a society where we are surrounded with brands to which we have positive and negative associations. Children as well as adults are continuously exposed to, and engage with, brands in their everyday life. This can clearly be both a compulsive and a pleasurable process as in the comment below from a 17-year-old young man written on a questionnaire in the Consumption study in answer to the question 'What do you think the item you have bought says about you?'

'That I have to buy brand names and that I love to shop.'

Brands are important to so many because they allow the construction of meanings, both actively and passively and indicate the groups with which people wish to identify as well as signalling status through style. In addition, brands allow the achievement of consistency in a changing world since branded products sell themselves on the idea of consistent quality. Equally importantly, they allow the avoidance of products that produce identities that people do not wish to be associated with (the 'undesired self' - Hogg and Banister, 2001). The following quotes indicate how young people consider that simply wearing branded goods makes young people 'cool' and popular.

> RP:　'Okay. So, some people are cool are they?'
> Calvin: 'Yeah, some people think they are cool.'
> RP:　'Right. Do they think they are cool?'
> Calvin: 'No. (.)[1] Some people do. Some people don't. I just think I am ordinary.'
> RP: 'Right. How do people become cool? What do they do to become cool?'
> Calvin: 'They like (.) get Adidas designer clothes and show-off.'[2]

> Q: 'So to be cool and popular what do you have to do? Do you have to wear certain things?'
> A: 'Yeah you have to buy expensive clothes and makes.'
> Q: 'What like logos and things?'
> A1: 'Like Nike.'
> A2: 'Adidas.'
> A3: 'Moschino.'
> A4: 'And like Calvin Klein and –'
> A: 'To get people to like you and that. You have to have the best.'[3]

---

[1]　Short pause of less than a second.
[2]　Masculinities study.
[3]　Consumption study, group interview with 12-13 year olds in Milton Keynes.

In discussing the importance of brands to the construction of some people's identities, it is easy to gain the impression that they are equally important to all young people's constructions of their identities. However, in the questionnaire on the Consumption study, we asked young people why they had wanted something they had recently bought. We found that young men were more likely than young women to say that brands are important to them. Twelve-year-old boys almost all said that they bought items because of the brand name, whereas this was less frequently the case for 17 and 18-year-old young men. However, the older young men were still more likely than young women to say that they bought things because of their brand names. There were thus age and gender differences in the importance of brands to identities. In addition, many young people cannot afford to buy brands – although some who cannot do buy imitation brands. Others deliberately choose youth styles that eschew brands. (David Locher, 1998) found this in a participant observation and interview study of two 'industrial-hardcore' bands in the USA.

> 'I don't have anything on that's worth over twenty dollars, and that's like if you put it in a nice little pile. I look like a Salvation Army [a Christian organization that provides food and clothes to the poor] truck threw up on me, and that's how it should be.'
>
> Locher, 1998: p. 108

Reasons for buying particular things

Despite the importance of brands to many young people, young people often say that they bought something because they like it. This was evident on the young people's questionnaire answers as in the following examples.

> 'I like the song 'Teenage Dirtbag' because it represents my mood.'
> Male12 who had bought the CD 'Wheatus', £14.99

> 'I like the heel on them.'
> Female 13 (Shoes, £35.99)

'I like the music and the band, I can listen to it and relax.'
Female 17 (CD - American Hi-Fi, £12.99)

'This game is good to play, very enjoyable because as well as keeping me occupied, it provides lots of inspiration for me.'
Male 17 (PS2 Game 'Armoured Core 2', £15.99)

Young people divided by style

When it comes to style, it may seem that young people are free to choose any styles they like. This is, to some extent, true. For example, young people choose to fit into particular styles. However, studies of young people, style and consumption demonstrate that there are consequences to choice of style. Ardiss Storm-Mathiesen in Norway, for example, found that style affected young people's social position in relation to whether they were seen as style leaders, followers or trying too hard – something that had an impact on their status among their peers. Similarly, Hanne Haavind and Mette Gulbrandsen found that style and behaviour also affected peer relations among 10-13 year olds (Haavind, 2003).

Teasing between groups of young people is frequently based on clothing and music styles in affluent societies and so is connected to sub-cultural affiliations (e.g. Eder, 1995; Griffin, 1993; Haavind, 2003; Staunaes, in press). The following quotes come from two group interviews with groups of 17 year olds in the Consumption study –in Birmingham and in Milton Keynes in England. Both groups were asked about the different groups in their schools.

Girl: 'The Kevs and Skaters don't mix really at school - the boys. But the girls do. 'Cos all the Sharons go with the Rocker type of skaters - because I've got friends who are really good friends with Sharons and they are skaters. And you don't hold it against them that they are Sharons and they are rockers.'[4]

Q: '...Do people get picked on if they are in the wrong group if you haven't got the right clothes on?'
Girl: 'Course you do, you get that at school because you get that even in working places now don't you? ...'[5]

---

[4] Birmingham group.
[5] Mixed-gender Milton Keynes group.

Social class, ethnicity, gender and consumption

The place of consumption in young people's social groups is more complex than simply conferring identities on individuals and leading to some style groups being teased or teasing others. It is possible to see divisions of social class, ethnicity and gender in what young people have to say about their identities constructed through identities. The two extracts below come from the masculinities study and address social class differences in consumption.

Q: 'Do you think there are people at school who come from different backgrounds to you. Some that are richer some poorer?'

Don: 'Yeah, there are some people richer than me. Because they like in the school party people come in with Chinos on. Where my mum orders from the catalogue, she can't really like buy Chinos, the Jeans are £60 a time, the tops are about £50. So that's £110 for the top and jeans.'

RP: 'Do people come in wearing that stuff do they?'

Don: 'Yeah, the school disco. I like the clothes I have. Girls wear (.) they like the clothes that I wear because I've got (.) jeans and an orange stripe top.'

RP: 'The boys that come in the Chino gear how do they make you feel then, how do you feel about that?'

Don: 'I don't feel any different. And they go, 'Oh what's that name brand you're wearing? I've got Calvin Klein on.'

Don: 'I say, 'Oh no', they go 'Western Trading what's that?'

RP: 'Do you think they feel superior to you then?'

Don: 'Yeah, I just say to them look as long as I wear good clothes, as long as I've got a decent pair of clothes and trainers it really don't matter what name brand it is. I think I wear brand things. I wear Reebok trainers I've got a pair of Kickers. They were £85. I've got a nice uniform and for my next birthday I'm going to get like a Calvin Klein Jumper, tee shirt and pair of socks and Calvin Klein Jeans.'[6]

RP: 'Is it boys (.) lower class boys who waste their money?'

Mathew: 'Yeah. On sort of expensive shoes, expensive tee-shirts (.) you know silly things which cost a lot.'

RP: 'Yeah.'

---

[6]   14-year-old white boy in the masculinities study.

Mathew: 'Cos they want (.) they want to look (.) as if they're not (.) lower class (.) and sort of (.) upper (.) so it's lo- (.) so people look at them and say, 'Oh wow they must be really rich because they have all these really expensive clothes' (.) but most of the time they've just wasted all their money (.) on buying this one set of clothes (.) and they sort of (.) wear them all the time.'
RP: 'What about middle class boys, do they (.) not wear designer clothes?'
Mathew: 'Well you don't (.) I, I sort of don't really need to (.) cos (.) I don't need to prove a point (2)[7] and I could if I wanted to but I don't want to because I (.) cos if you (.) if you wear designer clothes then you're constantly cautious (.) not to go and play football or not to do this or not to do that (.) cos you don't want.to get them dirty or anything. [RP: Mm] So I just sort of (.) not wear just normal clothes.'[8]

Don in the first extract above indicates that he would love to belong within his peer group but is struggling against exclusion because he does not have the economic resource to be able to consume what has become an important symbol of inclusion for the peer group. At the same time, he is clearly constructing himself as a member of the peer group. He is, therefore, defining himself as belonging to the peer group and struggling to define himself in ways that would allow him to be included. In a similar way, Mathew in the second extract defines himself in contrast to the 'lower classes'. He claims a more individual and superior position for himself, in ways that implicitly tell the interviewer that he considers himself middle class. His view of consumption also fits with (Bourdieu's, 1984) notion that the middle classes draw distinctions of taste between themselves and the working classes.

The following quote also comes from the Masculinities study and demonstrates how ethnicity is also present in young people's constructions of style.

Jamie: 'White people have their own styles so do black people (.) sometimes Moroccans have theirs (1) but Somalis just copy.'
RP: 'What's the white style then?'

---

[7] Brackets with a number indicate the length of a longer pause.
[8] 13-year-old white middle class boy in the masculinities study.

Dorin: 'Kind of normal in't it (Bill: tracksuit) (.) normal clothes (2) no flashness no nothing.'
RP: 'No flashness?'
Bill: 'Casual clothes.'
RP: 'So black boys are more flash are they than white boys?'
Bill: 'Yeah, they like showing off.'
RP: 'Why do the Somalis and Moroccans try and copy the black boys and not the white boys? (3).'
Jamie: 'It's just that (1) they learn that (.) the clothes that look (1) the (.) top in'it?'
Bill: 'I- I wouldn't wear them=[9]
Dorin: '=Black people they wear like, like design designer wear (2).'
RP: ' Right.'
Dorin: 'And like they (Lenny: more expensive) yeah much more expensive.'
RP: 'More expensive yeh?'
Bill: 'Yeh=.'
Jamie: '=Doesn't mean they've got more money or nothing it's just that (.) they like (.) they like to show what they've got and everything but (1) (RP: Right) they're just spending their money just on clothes.'[10]

The young men in the extract above draw distinctions between themselves as white and black people. In doing so, they are expressing solidarity on the basis of white people's consumption and claiming identities that they construct as preferable to Somali and black young men's, which they construct as undesirable. This claim is complicated since many white young men in the masculinities study gave accounts that indicated that black boys were the most popular boys who were most hegemonically masculine and were admired and envied by white boys (Frosh et al., 2002). One way in which white boys dealt with it was to denigrate black boys and, in the extract above, this is done through the decrying of consumption and style.

The following quote from the Consumption study is of a group of boys talking about girls' consumption of fashion.

---

[9] '=' denotes interruption by another respondent.
[10] Group interview, 14-year-old white young men in the masculinities study.

Boy 1: 'When you see a few people wear (.) people you know are persuaded by it and then (.) people all our age get it then the next thing you know is it's gone round so.'
Int: 'And then it's no good is it?'
Boy 2: 'Then you have to start another one (.) and then (1) and then that goes fashion goes on for about a week and then another fashion will start (inaudible) (1) fashion just seems to go round (1) so quick so.'
Boy 4: 'They don't last long.'
Int: 'And is it the same for girls? (1) I mean=.'
B4: '=I'd say girls are worst.'
Int: 'Worse?'
B6: 'Yeah (1) they'd spend more money on stuff.'
B1: 'If they go to a party and that they have to go out and buy a new outfit just to go to one party (1) when they're never going to go to another party like that or whatever they still have to wear an outfit for.'
Int: 'Just to be -.'
B5: 'They go out on a Friday they go out on a Saturday and they buy an outfit for each day (.) every week.'
B3: 'And perfumes.'
B6: 'And perfume they need a bottle of perfume just to go out I cant smell like it did last week.'
Int.: 'They should smell different should they as well as look different?'
B4: 'So (1) that boy might recognise it kind of thing one of you (.) so they (1) I reckon they would spend more money than us.'
B3: 'I think they're probably influenced more by celebrities [*some transcript omitted here*] Where I would like (inaudible) (1) I'd say get a couple of different kinds of jeans maybe (1) and then I would have a (1) black pair of shoes to go with it (.) I would just have one pair of black shoes and polish 'em up (.) but they but they'll have about three or four) this one has got to match this trouser. These shoes have got to match this trouser and this top (.) it's everything has got to match you've got to have a new outfit for everything. I'd say girls are a bit worse when it comes (.) to spending money.'[11]

---

[11] Boys' group interview, 17 year olds.

In the extract above, the boys in the group interview together construct a position for young women as trivial in their consumption practices and as easily influenced to follow ideas that their cycles of consumption should be short lived.

All the above quotes provide an indication that social divisions in society are part of young people's consumption experiences and important to the ways in which they position themselves in their peer group. They indicate that consumption is a symbolic process that is important to young people's identities and to divisions between them. The quotes show that the young people are acutely aware of differences in consumption based on choice of style group, social class, ethnicity, gender and age. Such differences are socially important and are often antagonistic.

Consumption and transactions between children and parents

Not surprisingly, most children are dependent on their parents for access to resources for consumption. In recent years, much attention has been given to the idea of 'pester power'. This relates to the perceived influence on children of advertising and, in consequence their nagging of their parents into buying goods (including foodstuff, clothes and toys) for them. (The British National Family and Parenting Institute, 2004) conducted research on what made their family life harder than it needed to be, what worried them and how they felt about raising children in twenty-first century Britain. A high percentage of the parents they interviewed (84%) said that companies targeted their children too much with marketing, that it was being targeted at younger ages and that they felt that it was their responsibility to exercise restraint on their children's demands, but that they could not reduce their children's exposure to advertising – e.g. on the internet and mobile phones. This is clearly an important issue and one at the heart of concerns that young children are increasingly likely to be obese. However like many issues concerned with consumption this issue has moral and political dimensions and is subject to debate and disagreement. While recognizing and taking seriously these concerns, however, it is worth looking at the broader context of transactions between parents and children over consumption.

One important aspect of the transactions between parents and children concerns that fact that, as birthrates have fallen in affluent countries, so children have become what some call 'trophy children' who are seen to reflect on their parents' identities and affluence.

(Prendergarst and Wong, 2003) conducted a study in Hong Kong to ask:

'Why do some parents buy luxury brands of clothing for their infants, when in fact their infants are too young to appreciate Armani, Versace, and other such labels? Are the parents doing this to impress others?'

p. 157

They first interviewed seven mothers, then conducted a short questionnaire survey of 134 mothers, recruited from Hong Kong shopping malls, who had purchased luxury brands of clothing for their infants found that parents say that they are motivated by the good quality and design associated with the luxury brands. They eschewed the notion conspicuous consumption as a route to impressing others as the main motivation. However, interviewees who spent more on luxury clothing brands for their infants were also determined to be more materialistic. It may, of course, be that mothers were reluctant to think of themselves as using their children as 'trophy children' and the question of why there has been an increase in the market in designer products requires more attention. However, parents clearly play an important part in children's consumption that is not entirely due to what the children themselves want.

Beyond infancy, children's markets have increased enormously in size as has children's active participation in consumption. In a small-scale ethnographic British study of 6-12 year old children's consumption, (Boden, Pole, Pilcher and Edwards, 2004) found that the children have images of themselves that they come into play in relation to their shopping. In keeping with (the National Family and Parenting Institute, 2004) findings, they also mentioned the influence of the peer group and advertising on what their children asked for and felt that they had to attempt to educate their children about responsible consumption. Nonetheless, they also recognised that children are under pressure from their peers to buy brand names etc. (Pole, 2004) suggests that parents recognised that, in the school context, what most people would see as 'wants' are 'needs' for their children if they are not to be teased by their peer group (in the ways Blatchford, 1998, found in his study of children's playground behaviour). These issues were also raised by parents in the consumption study on 12-13 year olds and 17-18 year old young people and their parents - from which the quote in the previous study comes. The following account was given by a mother of three daughters aged 9, 12 and 15 years.

> 'It's quite hard for young people to become accepted by their peer group. Consumption is part of that – part of their acceptance. By buying the same things – clothes and music – hopefully they're showing that they're part of a group and will be accepted by it... Now I think about it, it's happening at a younger age. She's 15, but the 12 year old now says 'If you don't buy this for me, then they won't be friends with me.' The 15-year old is not becoming more confident about being a little different... Strangely enough, they feel that school uniforms remove some of those pressures. It's 12-14 that is the hardest age for conformity I think. They remind me of something I saw on television, one young person wearing a tee shirt saying 'I'm an individual', then the camera pans back and everybody is wearing the same tee shirt. That's the contradiction they face – how to be an individual and be accepted as part of the group.'

This quote neatly encapsulates several important elements of consumption for young people's identities and negotiation with their parents. First, consumption is a useful symbolic resource for allowing young people to demonstrate that they belong to their peer group and so allows the negotiation of inclusion. However, it also positions them contradictorily between wanting to be individual and wanting to be accepted within a particular group. The ways in which this happens changes over time as well as developmentally. It is obviously important not to fall into the trap of extrapolating from one account to general social processes. The above quote fits with what parents say in other studies and helps us to understand why it is that parents are prepared to buy their children brand names, for example, even if they have little money available. For example, a quantitative British study by (Middleton et al., 1997) found that one per cent of children do not have a bed and mattress to themselves, five per cent live in damp housing and do not have access to fresh fruit each day or new shoes that fit. More than ten per cent of children over the age of 10 share a bedroom with a sibling of the opposite sex. Yet, counter-intuitively, over half the children who were defined as 'not poor' had parents who were defined as 'poor'. Their parents reported that they sometimes went without clothes, shoes and entertainment in order to make sure that their children are provided for. One in twenty mothers reported that they sometimes go without food in order to provide for their children. Alone mothers were particularly likely to report this for clothes for their daughters.

It must also be recognized that children sometimes influence their parents' consumption decisions. Most children are given some say over, for example, the food bought. Children thus have some, limited, influence over household resources (Beatty and Talpade, 1994; Gunter and Furnham, 1998). However, in a Swedish study, (Ekström, 1995) found that parents sometimes learn new aspects of purchasing and consumption from their children. Children both gave their parents information about what they should purchase and also helped them to install or use the products purchased (e.g. mobile phones, computers). She also found that children could help parents to become aware of products. Ekström calls this a 'keeping up with the children effect" (similar to 'keeping up with the Joneses'). In a previous study in Russia, Ekström encountered the idea of "the child as dictator". However, in her Swedish study the consumption relation between some parents and children seemed to be more like a friendship relation than a parent-child relationship – particularly in one-parent families-when they discussed purchases and consumption. Ekström reports that a Danish psychologist, Bent Hougaard uses the term 'curling parents' to describe parents who feel guilty enough about their children to make a lot of concessions to them. However, she sometimes found that parents could resist children's attempts to influence their consumption behaviour by doing the opposite.

It is also important to recognize that children are not only self-centred in their seeking of resources from their parents. Many children whose parents have low incomes are careful not to be a drain on their household resources. Indeed, even young children can learn that there are constraints on the money available. For example, (Walkerdine and Lucey, 1989) present an example of a four-year-old girl learning that she and her mother have to wait to go shopping until her father comes home with his pay packet. (Chin, 2001) found that black 10-year-olds in the USA living in poverty were extremely considerate about their parents' inability to buy things and never 'pestered' their parents for money to buy things (see the quote above). Child-parent negotiations about household resources are, therefore, likely to differ with the money available and how it is allocated within households (Brannen and Wilson, 1987; Ringen and Halpin, 1997; Beatty and Talpade, 1994). The two quotes below come from the Consumption study.

> Int: 'Do you mind if you can't have all the latest things?'
> B3: 'Yeah, course I do!'
> (Been brought up that way).
> B1: 'Anyone does, I'm just like yeah so!'
> G1: 'Yeah, I'm not (1) I have a rep! (Laughs) Yeah, coz if you don't have all the latest stuff (B1: = it like they just yeah) I know my mum can't afford it so I whenever, when I'm down, like, like when I was with you once its like you're not cool, look your clothes.'
> G2: 'You're just cast as the rejects really you're in the rejects pile.'[12]

> 'I think it's quite patronising actually because at 17 and 18 and your parents are still giving you pocket money (.) They like giving you a balance every week (.) I think it's just like invading your own space (.) your own will to go out and do something (.) but if you get it (.) um (.) spoon fed then you won't want to go out and get it yourself (.) you just stay home for the rest of your life getting it given to you...'[13]

In the first quote above, the young people indicate that parents' lack of resources have a direct impact on young people's status. They agreed that they would like to be able to have 'the latest things', but one young woman explains that her mother cannot afford to buy her such things and another agrees that those who cannot afford such things are 'rejects'. However, the young people do not suggest that they will 'pester' their parents for resources, but instead appear to accept that their parents do not have the necessary money. The second quote, produced by a young man from a working class family, demonstrates the construction of a worldview that makes 'pestering' parents unacceptable. He proposes a philosophy that suggests that it is patronising for parents to spoon-feed their older teenagers by giving them things they haven't worked for. This philosophy problematizes young people who 'pester' their parents for money.

There is evidence that some young people do 'pester' their parents for money for consumption as in the following two quotes.

---

[12] Mixed group of 12-13 year olds from a MK school serving impoverished estate.

[13] Working class young man, 17-year-old.

G1: 'My sister is more demanding than I am (.) and like if (.) she wants something she'll keep going on and on about it, so mum's finally gives in and gets it her and then we're broke for the rest of the week she's got to learn to understand that my mum hasn't got a lot of money.'[14]

I: 'Erm do you think that there are pressures on parents to buy certain things = F2: = Yeah = = for young people? You do?'
F2: 'Yeah.'
I: 'What kind of pressures?'
F2: ''Cos 'erm when you're working with young kids you always see it like with the little kids you like you've got people saying 'oh my clothes are better than yours.'
I: 'Uh-huh.'
F2: 'And you got people who go they'll go home to parents and say 'oh so-and-so's just got new trainers and they're taking the Mickey out of mine can you go and get me some new one's?' like parents like going 'well I ain't got the money' 'oh please please' they beg and then parents go and get it ya.'
I: 'Right.'
F2: 'And you got some kids who are like really spoilt as well so.'
I: 'Right that you see that in you're actual work?'
F2: 'Yeah.'
I: 'Do you think that happens sort of with people you're age at all or do you think it's just with younger?'
F2: 'I think it's just really mostly with the younger generation but some people like take it to like when they're older anyway.'
I: 'Right.'
F2: 'They still get spoilt.'
I: 'Right.'
F2: 'And like because like the parents have bought them everything anyway they - they end up thinking they can have everything they want until like they're at work.'[15]

In both the above examples, there are hints of a developmental trajectory in that the young woman in extract one says that her sister will have to 'learn to understand' that her mother does not have much

____

[14] 12 year old - mainly working class Milton Keynes school.
[15] Group of five white, Year 12 girls in Birmingham – four aged 16 years and one aged 17 years.

money. In the second extract one girl (F2) builds up a case about 'little kids' and says that it is mostly (but not only) the 'younger generation' who pester their parents. Both accounts also show how the amount of money available (and social class) impacts on transactions between parents and children. Implicitly (in the first extract) or explicitly (in the second extract) there is an engagement with the notion that some parents are under pressure from some children to buy them consumer goods.

Both sets of speakers clearly exonerate themselves from being children who pressure their parents about consumption. The implication is that they are individuals who are not so influenced by their peers that they pressure their parents. They, therefore, position themselves outside that aspect of youth culture and in disapproval of it. The young woman in the second extract says 'you get some kids who are like really spoilt'. Overall, there is no sympathy with the pressures that may cause young people to pester their parents. Yet, the speaker in the second extract acknowledges that 'little kids' make unfavourable comparisons with other children's clothes and tease them. This fits with (Bourdieu's, 1984) notion that distinctions of taste are common. (Peter Blatchford's, 1998) work on bullying in school would indicate that teasing of this sort is so difficult to bear that it makes understandable some children's attempts to persuade their parents into giving them money to buy brand-name clothing. (Karin Ekström's, 1995) research and the research by Middleton et al., also provide indications that some parents are sensitive to this and so may be prepared to go without things themselves in order to buy things for their children.

A question that is raised, rather than answered by the first extract is what leads the younger sister who is the subject of the quote to wheedle money from her mother when (Elizabeth Chin, 2002) found that the poor black 10 year olds she studied in the USA did not. This may well result from cultural differences or the fact that the children Elizabeth Chin studied are not unusual in their neighbourhood, whereas the sister being discussed may feel excluded from belonging to her peer group by lack of resources. It is also important to remember that, in both extracts, we hear about the wheedling from outsiders to those transactions. In the first extract it is a close family and household member who is being discussed, so it is possible to argue that this is part of the speaker's experience. However, in the second case, the issues discussed are further removed from the speaker's experience. Nonetheless, the ways in which both accounts are constructed indicate that consumption is important to identities in that consumption produces insiders and outsiders in relation to the status that young people achieve through consumption.

Conclusion

This chapter has argued that, for young people, consumption is an important way in which they can construct desired identities for themselves. The consumption of brand names in particular allows young people (and adults) to project desired identities and avoid the undesired self. In addition, 'digital technology' affects young people's identities. However, consumption is not only a process affecting individuals and young people's consumption is important to their peer group membership. Young people's consumption involves them in learning to manage peer relationships of solidarity and conflict and in negotiating societal differences, e.g. of gender, ethnicity and social class.

References

Abrams, M. (1959); *The Teenage* Consumer. London: Press Exchange.

Beatty, Sharon and Salil Talpade (1994); Adolescent Influence in Family Decision Making: A Replication with Extension. *Journal of Consumer Research 21* (September): 332-341.

Blatchford, P. (1998); *Social Life in School: Pupils' experience of breaktime and recess from 7 to 16 years*. London: Falmer.

Boden, S., C. Pole, J. Pilcher and T. Tim Edwards (2004); *New Consumers? The Social and Cultural Significance of Children's Fashion*. Paper presented to the Children as Consumers: Public Policies, Moral Dilemmas, Academic Perspectives Seminar, Friday 20 February 2004, Royal Society, London.

Bourdieu, P. (1984) (1979); *Distinction: A Social Critique of the Judgement of Taste*. Trans. R Nice. London: Routledge.

Brannen, J. and G. Wilson (1987); Introduction, in Brannen, J. and G. Wilson (Eds.), *Give and Take in Families: Studies in resource distribution*. London: Allen and Unwin.

Chin, E. (2001); *Purchasing Power: Black Kids and American Consumer Culture*. Minneapolis: University of Minnesota Press.

Eder, D. (1995); *School Talk: Gender and Adolescent Culture*. New Brunswick: Rutgers University Press. (With C. Evans and S. Parker).

Ekström, Karin M. (1995); *Children's Influence in Family Decision Making; A Study of Yielding, Consumer Learning and Consumer Socialization*. Göteborg: Bas ek.för.

Foucault, M. (1977); *Discipline and Punish*. Tavistock, London.

Frosh, Stephen, Ann Phoenix and Rob Pattman (2002); *Young Masculinities. Understanding boys in contemporary society*. Houndmills: Palgrave.

Furby, L. (1978); Possessions: toward a theory of their meaning and function throughout the life cycle, in P. B. Baltes (ed), *Life Span Development and Behavior*, Vol. 1, pp. 297-336. New York: Academic Press.

Griffin, Chris (1993); *Representations of Youth: The study of youth and adolescence in Britain and America*. Cambridge: Polity.

Gunter, B. and A. Furnham (1998); *Children as Consumers: A Psychological Analysis of the Young People's Market*. London: Routledge.

Haavind, Hanne 2003 (b); Masculinity by rule-breaking: Cultural contestations in the transitional move from being a child to being a young male. *NORA: Nordic Journal of Women's Studies, 11, (2)* 89-100.

Hogg, M. and E. Banister (2001); Dislikes, distastes and the undesired self: Conceptualising and exploring the role of the undesired end state in consumer experience. *Journal of Marketing Management, 17,* pp. 73-104.

Langager, S. (2004); Strange alliances on the threshold of the digital age. *Nordisk Pedagogik*, 24,56-69.

Locher, D. (1998); The industrial identity crisis: The failure of a newly forming subculture to identify itself, in J. Epstein (ed.), *Youth Culture: Identity in a Postmodern World*. Oxford: Blackwell.

Middleton, S., K. Ashworth and I. Braithwaite (1997); *Small Fortunes: spending on children, childhood poverty and parental sacrifice*.York: Joseph Rowntree Foundation.

Miles, S. (2000); *Youth Lifestyles in a Changing World*. Buckingham: Open University Press.

Miles, S, D. Cliff and V. Burr (1998); Fitting in and sticking out': Consumption, consumer meanings and the construction of young people's identities. *Journal of Youth Studies, 1,1*: 81-91.

National Family and Parenting Institute (2004); *Hard Sell, Soft Targets?* London: NFPI.

Pole, C. (2004); *Comment on Karin Ekström's lecture Consumer Kids: Competent or Victimized*. 20 February, The Royal Society, London.

Prendergast, G. and C. Wong (2003); Parental influence on the purchase of luxury brands of infant apparel: an exploratory study in Hong Kong. *Journal of Consumer Marketing, 20 (2)*, pp . 157-169.

Rheingold, H. (2002); *Smart Mobs: The next social revolution*. New York: Perseus Publishing.

Ringen, Stein and Brendan Halpin (1997); Children, Standard of Living and Distributions in the Family. *Journal of Social Policy* 26:21-41.

Sherry, J. F. (1998); The Soul of the Company Store: Nike Town Chicago and the Emplaced Brandscape, in J.F. Sherry (ed.), *The Concept of Place in Contemporary Markets*. Chicago: NTC Publishing.

Staunaes, D. (in press); From culturally avantgarde to sexually promiscuous – troubling intersections of age, femininity, whiteness and ethnicity. *Feminism and Psychology. Nordic special issue.*

Storm-Mathisen, A. (1998); *Buying pressures - what is that? A preliminary project on the meaning of clothing among 13-year-olds.* Report 4:96 Oslo: Statens Institutt for Forbruksforskning.

Walkerdine, V. and H. Lucey (1989); *Democracy in The Kitchen.* London: Virago.

Widdicombe, S. and R. Wooffitt (1995); *The Language of Youth Subcultures: Social identity in action.* Hemel Hempstead: Harvester Wheatsheaf.

5

Children and Promotion: The Role of Advertising and Marketing in Innovation

BRIAN YOUNG

Advertising to children and innovation

Some of you might wonder why the literature on advertising and marketing to children should be covered in a chapter of a book on innovation by children and adolescents. There may be several reasons why advertising has a significant role to play in innovation but the main one would be related to the cycle of consumption. In order to do justice to this concept and in particular the vital and essential role that advertising and marketing play within it we shall borrow a couple of concepts from that great Swiss developmental psychologist, Jean Piaget. Piaget used the ideas of assimilation and accommodation in his writings and leant heavily on their biological origins when describing them (Flavell, 1963: p. 44ff). Let's start with the infant who's playing with a pack of sweets with a brightly coloured portrayal of *Homer Simpson* on it. She can **accommodate** to the packaged good by grasping it, perhaps laughing at the familiar character that's she's seen on TV or on the supermarket shelves, and will show signs of distress if Mum tries to take it away. Mum can respond in different ways and might yield and even help her eat by removing the wrapper with Homer on it. Or Mum might be stricter – perhaps because her own experience as a child or within her family taught her never to give into a child's desires or the child will grow up with a weak character – and take away the sweets replacing them with a piece of fruit, because she read about 'how to be a good parent' in her favourite magazine. So there are different styles of socialisation and these can emerge from sources such as cultural traditions within families or media sources like magazines. The child at this stage has a limited repertoire of behaviours or ways of **assimilating** objects in the environment. These assimilatory structures or **schemata** will develop over time and in interaction with the environment. Maybe later on when the infant is wheeled round the supermarket in a shopping trolley she will interact actively with the parent and request various goods by crying, attracting attention and making purchase requests with the limited communicative repertoire that is available at that age. Later on children will develop more language and cognitive skills so that commercial communications such as advertising or promotions in the supermarket will be recognised as such and will be seen to be there to try and get you to buy them. In addition children will develop an understanding of money and be given an allowance and become an active economic actor, budgeting and purchasing and saving. This span of development from infancy to adolescence, just part of the great trajectory of life from conception to death, is guided by the two main aspects of adaptation which Piaget called assimilation and accommodation and taken together they drive change in the child. We can see then that the cycle of consumption relies on all the different forms of representation of goods and services that are there in the child's environment and the way the child accommodates to them using the strengths and limitations of the schemata that are there to assimilate them, is consumption in the broadest possible sense. A developmental approach to consumption is not just an ancillary aspect of consumer psychology or consumer behaviour – the chapter that deals with kids and youth or that maybe gets a mention when ethical issues is tagged on as an afterthought – but it can provide a widening context that raises interesting and challenging issues about the very nature of consumption itself. In addition we've all been there and there's no way of escaping our own histories as we grew up.

It's also important to define the representation of goods and services as widely as possible because young children who don't understand why commercial communications are there will not necessarily make the distinction between different forms of intent behind the communication nor will they realise the economic and financial context within which these communications operate. So there's no point in working with a definition of advertising that limits the goods and services so portrayed to only those that involve communications that are paid for and that are intentionally aimed at different sectors of a market as young children will not recognise this and other equally influential representations that are culturally available will be neglected. A developmental psychology approach to consumption and commercial communications needs to identify all the contexts in which the child may be exposed to and may find representations of goods and services, irrespective of whether they were intentionally put there as part of the economic activity of marketing. A rather dusty and worn pack of sweets with Homer Simpson on them found in a schoolbag, a TV ad for them, a supermarket shelf where they are displayed, and a TV programme called *The Simpsons* that the family watch are all equally valid occurrences of that branded good. If we assume that children make sense of their environment as their own mental schemata develop and that part of this development relies on exposure to and assimilation of these representations, each occurrence has a potential impact.

Innovation can be seen as a style of consumption for particular goods and services and this style will have emerged as a product of many different factors of influence. Innovation suggests responsive and change by children to change itself and representations of goods and services have an important role to play. For example, much attention has been paid recently to the precursors of materialism in children and the extent to which one is materialistic or not could constitute a core set of values that drives an interest in goods and services, an involvement in communications about them, and an intention to buy them or persuade others to do so. A recent theory of materialism (Kasser et al., 2004) has assumed that materialism or rather a materialistic value orientation (MVO) is largely influenced by the trappings of a capitalistic free-market economy with the extensive promotion of different kinds and brands of goods and services:

> 'Research suggests two main pathways toward the development of an MVO. First, experiences that undermine the satisfaction of psychological needs can cause individuals to orient toward materialism as one type of compensatory strategy intended to countermand the distressing effects of feelings of insecurity. Second, materialistic models and values exert more direct influences on the development of an MVO through the process of socialization, internalization, and modeling'.
>
> Op. cit., p13

In other words living in a material world is not only psychologically unhealthy as it induces feelings of low self-worth and insecurity but as we grow up in that world we learn quite quickly to aspire to acquire such goods and services which are held in such high esteem by famous and attractive role models. The processes involved in the latter include modelling and upward social comparison. Advertising is seen by Kasser et al. as part of the cultural mix that endorses the good materialistic life but media in general with game shows such as *The Price is Right* and *Who Wants to Be a Millionaire?* are also seen to be celebrating the virtues rather than the vices of materialism. Children soon learn to become part of this world and hold these values.

Changing media

The media landscape where promotion and marketing to children can be found is rapidly changing and is virtually unrecognisable from that of 20 years or even 10 years ago. At the time of writing the average household in Europe or the United States or in several cities in Asia has many access points to enter the world of communications. If we take a household with children then they will have more than one TV set with a set in the main living room and one in the child's room. There will be a telephone with a landline and possibly a dedicated line for Net use. Mobile phone use by children is increasing and in the UK whereas only 22% of children aged 9-10 years use mobile phones, this figure has increased to over 60% for 11-12-year-olds (Jones, 2002). There are cross-national differences however and many countries in Europe, where the geography is more conducive to cell phone coverage than in the US, have remarkably high figures for mobile phone ownership. (Powell and Wicken, 2002) for example compared survey data in the US and the UK and whereas only 44% of 12-17 year olds in the US owned or used mobile phones, the equivalent figure for the UK was 75%. Many urban households in Europe and many more in the US have cable feeds for hundreds of TV channels or have installed satellite dishes that can receive various bundles of TV transmissions at different subscription rates. A computer with Internet capabilities and storage devices that include CD-ROM and DVD is available in many homes. The television receiver will no doubt be linked to a video-recorder (VCR) and perhaps nowadays a DVD player. There are other forms of storage like TiVo, a solid state store that affords instant playback and smart memory to prompt the user to record frequently viewed programme categories at the touch of a button. There is a growth in digital television with an associated interactive capability and choice of camera angle at sporting events. What used to be known as 'MTV' is now a generic category for many branded channels some with interactive capability such as viewer voting onscreen for the most popular music videos. Children use the Net frequently. A six-year study on Internet use by children (79% from the United States) showed that a quarter of children in 2001 can be classified as 'heavy users'

> '...Spending ten hours or more online each week - up from an average of just 19% for the previous four years'.
>
> Clarke, 2002: p. 45

Advertising is carried on television of course but branded products in attractive contexts can also appear in videogames and the Internet will carry advertising too where it is more difficult to avoid than TV spot advertising. SMS advertising using mobile phones is used with older children. Branding is used more and more in children's clothes and in general the child lives in a 'branded environment'.

Marketing strategies to children have also changed and it is common practice for new brands to be launched on the back of other media representations. So what is effectively being promoted is the brand that adds value to other acts of consumption. Eating out at *McDonalds* is tied into a *Disney* film by promotional packages and toys. And the settings for both these events will in all probability be close to each other with the growth of out-of-town centres with drive-in and eat-in burger food next to a multiplex cinema so the behaviours and the character endorsers become inextricably entwined in promotion and in behaviour. *Spider-Man* and *Pokémon* make regular branded appearance on TV, movies, computer games, web sites, toys, food, and clothing so the original referent of the brand becomes confused with the secondary ones. Word-of-mouth or 'viral' marketing hijacks one of processes of innovation by identifying cool kids on the block and giving them free products to distribute (Siegel, Coffey and Livingstone, 2001).

> 'O what a tangled web we weave/when first we practise to deceive!'
>
> Scott, 1806

In summary…

… We have seen that adopting a developmental approach to children, consumption, and various forms of marketing and promotion can be a project that is theoretically interesting and conceptually integrated. Not only does this avoid the marginalisation of 'ads and kids' as a separate chapter in a textbook or as an illustration in good (or bad) business ethics but it can provide a broader context within which to view and conceive of branded environments, culture, and change as a consequence of development. Adult consumers were children too and the acquisition of preferences, values, and interests that drive our styles of consumption whether of goods and services or commercial communications has a history, both as we grow and develop as individuals and as our cultures change. The media landscape has changed and boundaries between brand and product become vague as well as spot advertising being only one of an increasing variety of marketing strategies and media platforms for marketing to children. But children and advertising have other qualities and we shall now look at the extent to which different issues emerge and how they can be looked at from different academic vantage points.

The following list is by no means inclusive and I'm sure that readers will be able to add to it from their own experience in their own country and that future readers who pick this volume up from the Internet shelves of an electronic library will be able to add to it such is the pace of technological advance both in media and in commercial communications. But the 'issues' in advertising to children are not just dry academic ways of carving up a particular research 'field'. They arise when popular opinion, exploited it must be said by politicians who see a certain advantage to be gained by adopting positions of moral outrage, is sparked by change or dispute that hits the headlines. So the recent rise in obesity and the World Health Organisation's (WHO) warnings of a pandemic worldwide (WHO, 2000; WHO, 2003) would suggest that advertising of so-called junk food to children and its role as a contributory factor will be an issue and at the time of writing it certainly is. When I started my own research in this area in the 1980s I was funded by the Health Education Council (HEC) in the UK and my brief was to look at advertising of sugared foods to children in the context of influences on dental caries with that population. That was an issue at the time but a close look at (WHO, 2003) reveals only a passing reference to this issue at the beginning of the 21st century. Issues and public anxieties come and go, suggesting that there is a cyclical quality to these concerns and maybe just a whiff of 'moral panic'. So here is my list.

Advertising in schools

This has emerged recently an issue in the USA although it's not particularly seen as a problem in the UK. The recent APA report on advertising to children (Kunkel et al., 2004) stated that

> 'Advertising in schools has grown so extensively that we have prepared a separate report to document these changes and to explore the issues they raise'.
>
> Palmer et al., 2004, op.cit., p. 3

Dental health/diet/obesity

I have included these concerns as one although dental matters seem to have lessened recently in the light of the obesity pandemic. They are intimately related to food advertising and are related to an associated set of concerns to do with 'what's on'. The most recent and best known review in this area was published by the Food Standards Agency (FSA) in the UK (Hastings et al., 2003).

What's on?

This is a perennial problem to do with the content of advertising and promotion directed at children. Content analyses of food advertising in particular have been conducted at regular intervals (see Gamble and Cotugna, 1999) and other concerns have included the body image portrayed by actors in TV ads (excessively and unattainably slim) as well as materialistic and aspirational messages that consumption brings popularity. I have kept these concerns separate from whether children are actually influenced to think and feel differently as a consequence of watching all this material, although the difference is often not recognized in some of the more polemical arguments in the area. Another assumption is that there's too much of it and that's not good. So we have figures cited of how many TV ads the average child is exposed to each year that preface most general articles on advertising to children. The current quote for the USA is 40,000 commercials annually on television (Kunkel, 2001). Often this figure goes along with an estimate of either how much the child market is worth or how much is spent on advertising to children. The latest figures are that children aged between 2 and 14 years influence purchases of about $500 billion annually and that the amount of money spent on marketing to children was $12 billion a year (cited in Levin and Linn, 2004: p. 213). Again the effect of these figures on children and how large they are compared with for example other forms of communication and influence is often neglected and the image of the child that is assumed is of a passive recipient of information where getting more means more harm inflicted.

Understanding intent

Advertising and promotional activity in general serves a variety of functions. Although the ultimate aim is to make the brand more profitable, usually by increasing or maintaining sales, there are several intermediate goals that often need to be achieved en route – without losing sight of the fact that the interests of the shareholders of the company, that is responsible for the brand, are paramount. So brands have to be visible and memorable and salient in a crowded market place and there will be jostling and hustling for a good position relative to a lucrative sector. As we have seen half a trillion US dollars is a lucrative market and as young children's attention and memory are driven very much by what they see and perceive rather than their knowledge of the contingencies of their environment and the accompanying schemata there is strong competition to make sensory vivid and attractive advertising to children. But children do not understand the purpose of advertising to the same extent as adults or adolescents and even if they do claim in self-report assessments to know the purpose behind advertising they cannot utilize and deploy that information under every set of circumstances (John, 1999). So knowing what knowledge children have about the intent of advertising - ranging from a simple naïve assumption that it's there because it's fun (with preschoolers) to a sophisticated understanding of the economic and political and social role that advertising has which may occur in some adolescents – is central to the debate about whether it's fair or unfair to advertise to children. I have explored this issue elsewhere (Young, 2002) in the context of advertising literacy and the various psycho-legal issues that emerge when the two groups of developmental psychologists and regulatory bodies attempt to answer this question of 'an age of consent' to advertising.

Effects and influence

I have used both expressions here as effects has a particular theoretical status in media research where a stimulus (advertising) is presumed to have an effect, mediated or not, at some level on a person whether it is on attitudes, feelings, moods or values; knowledge and beliefs; or intention to behave, or behaviour itself. This extended metaphor is extremely seductive and can often block out alternative ways of thinking about advertising such as the child as an active decision maker, operating in a collective nexus with peers, and utilizing various resources including advertising. In addition there are several concerns that are subsumed under the general heading of the effects or influence of advertising – not least; who is the recipient of these effects? Is it the family, or the child, or children? Effects can also be proximal or distal. So the child at home might see an ad for some crisps, know they are in the fridge, and go and get a pack. The mediators here between seeing the ad and doing something are quite simple and immediate – the ad prompts an action and, like all good crimes, there's a motive, a means, and an opportunity. That's a proximal effect. But other effects are cumulative and here the terminology should really be influence rather than effect as advertising has an influence amongst many others. So whether living in a branded environment increases the probability of children becoming more materialistic or if the ubiquitous 'obesigenic' environment can lead to fatness – these cannot be answered simply and we assume that there are various factors operative. We are some way toward understanding what these factors are and more importantly how they are structured. For example, borrowing a concept from the well-known research on the influence of violent media on aggressive behaviour we know that:

> 'Most researchers of aggression agree that severe aggressive and violent behavior seldom occurs unless there is a convergence of multiple predisposing and precipitating factors such as neurophysiological abnormalities, poor childrearing, socioeconomic deprivation, poor peer relations, attitudes and beliefs supporting aggression, drug and alcohol abuse, frustration and provocation, and other factors. The evidence is

already substantial that exposure to media violence is one such long-term predisposing and short-term precipitating factor.'

Huesmann and Skoric, 2003: p. 221

The above can provide a useful hypothesis generator and research model of the role of advertising in producing long-term effects on physical conditions such as obesity or value systems like materialism. But distal influence needs much more research if we are to be confident just how much influence advertising has overall and when it has an effect and when that effect is negligible.

Types of advertising

Finally there are issues surrounding different kinds of promotional activity to children. We've seen how food advertising has a particular research agenda surrounding it, and there are different concerns with toy advertising for example that are centered on the extent to which the reality as portrayed in the ad does not correspond to the reality of the toy car itself when the child plays with it. Or the images on the package provide a romanticised and unrealistic portrayal of the actual product. One would anticipate that items where the price is substantial and the purchase is not necessarily renewable over regular intervals are just those kinds of items where the match between representation and reality must be accurate and any mismatch would soon produce consumer dissatisfaction. Toys, especially those bought with money given as a birthday gift for example would be like this for young consumers. Fast moving consumer goods (fmcgs) on the other hand where trial purchase is to be expected and the consequences of dissatisfaction are easily coped with by brand switching, should not produce the same consumer regret. But one of the most dramatic turn rounds in the history of retail was the rise and fall of *Sunny Delight* which was marketed as a healthy orange drink for children, and the visual imagery in the promotional material and packaging as well as the location in the store supported that message, until consumer groups pointed out that the ingredients contained hardly any juice and were primarily sweeteners, colouring, and water. I suspect that this case study exemplified an important issue in consumer concern that is peculiar to food and it centers round the concern with added value especially when price bears little relationship to the value of the ingredients. But before we look at that – and the case of adding value to children's products by using celebrity endorsement in promotion – we need a model of 'junk food'.

Junk food!

The model I have used is based on a many-layered ball with a centre. At the centre are the ingredients and in many cases these are the least important aspect of the product. They might be sugar, starch, flavouring, and colouring. They are not the sorts of things one would go and buy in order to cook a food from raw ingredients as one would do if baking a cake for example. Value is added and in the trade these are know as 'high value added products'. There are two kinds of additions. One consists of the ingredients produced by food technologists that are seen as necessary in order for the product to survive in the market place. Because of the dominance of supermarkets and the global nature of food manufacturing, the scale of distribution networks require that foods are able to endure the journeys from field to checkout both en route and on shelves without any apparent change to their quality. Consumers believe they need the same experience every time they buy brand X and brand X must deliver this whether it's bright green peas or very sweet apples or in the case of high value added products, the same taste experience and similar post-ingestive and post-digestive consequences. I say 'believe they need the same taste experience' because some critics will argue consumers have been seduced by careful marketing to want or even desire sameness and that maybe difference should be desirable. In addition – and this is particularly relevant in the child market – the product should look attractive, even before the promotion and packaging. So ingredients are pulverized and squeezed into strange shapes and filled with air and colour is added so food becomes playful and fun.

It's important to mention that up until this point there has been no promotion and packaging added on to this multi-layered model of junk food. And yet there's enough in the transformation from the 'raw' to the 'cooked', to borrow a concept from the great anthropologist (Levi-Strauss, 1970) for people to complain about and they do. One of the advantages of having such a model is that it adds structure to the litany of whingeing and moaning that emerge when foods and kids are uttered in the same breath. Is it the transformation itself? Should food be natural? Why do we allow children to play with their food and have their food played with in this way? Food is serious and part of high culture. Supermarkets are symptomatic of the wildest excesses of rampant capitalism and we should all shop in farmers' markets and join the 'slow food' revolution. Why are companies allowed to make money from selling a penny's worth of raw ingredients? Mutton dressed as lamb (or worse)! Look at how much we pay at the checkout and how much the picker gets in Kenya. Do you know what actually goes into burgers?? And so on. My point is not that these criticisms are misplaced and I'm sure they aren't and that many people are genuinely worried that we have got ourselves to this state with one of the most sophisticated of all cultural inventions – cuisine – but that they have nothing to do with advertising and promotion but everything to do with how the foods we give to our children have gone way beyond the limited transformations of the days of pickling and preserving and alphabet soup or (in my own memories) making hills and rivers out of mashed potato and gravy!

But to return to packaging and promotion. One can imagine a cultural veneer being applied to an already valued added model of the layered sphere. When an object acquires cultural meaning then it is changed. According to cultural theorists who have written about advertising (e.g. Williamson, 1978) one of the characteristics of these changes is that the branded good is transported into the world of dreams, aspirations, and fantasy that is the land of advertising and promotion. The mundane and ordinary (and trivial) content of the food – the ingredients – are **transmuted** into something else, which is the snack food that is ingested but are also **transported** into a world where desires can be realised. This is the cultural product and is the end of the line. Now people might be worried and have anxieties about that because children are being seduced into believing that what they are going to get is not what is actually there or they might have an aesthetic dislike of the vulgarity of much advertising to children. But I would contend that these worries and concerns are far less problematic than the other concerns about 'what have they done to our food' and are also easier for me anyway to alleviate. For example much of what has been written about so-called advertising theory by cultural theorists is florid and opaque and uses a unique vocabulary that is sometimes more an extension of the pretensions of the author (e.g. Barthes, 1973) than a tool for explaining ideas. Consequently it is, for me, as a consumer of this sort of writing rather than a contributor, necessary to strip it down and redesign it – much to the chagrin no doubt of the original authors and their followers. I have found that images and metaphors usually do the job hence the 'layers of the onion' metaphor. However as a developmental psychologist I know and accept that children are capable of different levels of understanding and one of these is the extent to which they can keep separate the temptations of the land of magic where they often find stories and packages about the brand, from the reality of the stuff of the product whether they be crisps or sweets or whatever. This literacy is an important mediator that needs to be taken into account in discussing whether advertising and promotion to children is fair or not.

Celebrity endorsement

Adding a celebrity to a package or making an ad where a famous person acts out a theme with a brand or even establishing connections between characters (such as Disney's *The Lion King*) and a brand can be incorporated into our model by suggesting that the brand can benefit by accruing some value from the celebrity. In fact where tie-ins occur both parties will benefit from the mutual relationship. There is a similarity with the interpersonal impression management strategy known as 'basking in reflected glory' where one person attempts to raise his or her self-esteem by mixing socially with famous or especially talented people (Cialdini et al., 1976). I have developed the parallel between interpersonal communication and promotional communication elsewhere (Young, 2002) when talking about the similarity between performance at interviews for example and the 'promotional principle' that guides advertising.

Why is this technique seen as a problem with children? It seems to me symptomatic of the unease that people feel about allowing the child to enter a world of stories and fantasies where famous people or characters are identified with brands. This aversion can take various forms. For example *Walkers Crisps* in the UK use Gary Lineker, who used to be a soccer player and is now a sports commentator on TV, as a celebrity endorser. Gary is seen in various episodes of a narrative series of TV commercials, engaged in humorous vignettes that invariably show him eating and enjoying the brand (for more information, see the case study cited in the references under 'anon.'). Criticisms have been levelled at the association of ideas involved where the product (*Walkers Crisps*) is linked with a footballer on the grounds that crisps are unhealthy food whereas Gary is healthy and a footballer – although for today's audience of children he is more likely to be seen as 'someone on TV who talks about football'. There is also a concern that children might not understand what's going on and indeed some limited unpublished research that we have done at Exeter suggests that young children do not understand the role of endorser or promoter being taken by an actor and that they think Gary eats them because he likes them. I have no idea whether Mr. Lineker enjoys his work to the extent he appreciates and uses the product he endorses, but he need not and there must be a developmental psychology of acting and actors that could inform the debate. In fact the general research field of the child's understanding of different strategies and tactics in advertising is an under-researched area.

I'm sure there are other ways of identifying and allocating one's experience of issues in children and advertising under various heads and these are just the ones that I've come up with. My contribution in this chapter however was not intended to set out a research agenda just by highlighting subtopics in the field that I thought deserved some research treatment. The question would be: which particular empirical strategy or scholarly approach would be appropriate. Because, as I hinted in the section on a model for junk food, practitioners and writers in this area tend to come from a variety of backgrounds with a host of different assumptions and traditions of enquiry. As an eclectic consumer of ideas with a fairly robust approach to the carefully crafted work of others, I tend to borrow, beg and steal. I suspect I'm not alone and one of the strengths of consumer research is just that mixture of eclecticism and willingness to be open to new approaches. So in this last section I want to look at some of the different approaches to the study of advertising and marketing to children and try and combine them with the areas of content to generate a rich research agenda.

Approaching the subject

Empirical simulations

There are several studies, many of which are cited in the FSA Report (Hastings et al., op. cit.), that use a paradigm that is based on empirical studies where independent and dependent and mediating variables are defined and operationalised, and data is analysed using various correlational models, including multiple regression. The work of Goldberg (Goldberg et al., 1978; Gorn and Goldberg, 1982) falls into this area as does recent research linking television viewing and food consumption by children (Halford et al., in press; Borzekowski and Robinson, 2001). Although such work is to be welcomed as it is subject to the rigours of scientific evidence, what goes on in the microcosm of the laboratory need not generalise to the reality of children consuming media and goods in the real world. I have developed this critique elsewhere (Young et al., 1996; Young, 2004) but the main point is that although research findings from these studies have high internal validity, they have little or no external validity.

Cultural and anthropological approaches

When Russ Belk published his much-cited paper (Belk, Wallendorf and Sherry, 1989) on how shopping could be seen as the new religion, he leant heavily on the concept of 'sacred and profane' originally developed by Durkheim in the context of religion. Sacred objects are characterised by rites and prohibitions and there are ritualistic ways of dealing with them. Belk consumed the literature avidly and produced an eclectic approach to consumption. There is little of this kind of treatment of the children and television literature and yet it seems ripe for this sort of approach. I have attempted to make sense of the public anxieties that are often expressed when 'advertising' and 'children' are put together by arguing that these images are cast in the mould of the advertiser as seducer and the child as innocent – a relationship of mythic significance (Young, 1990). Perhaps there is a similar way of tackling the issue of advertising to children in schools. The school is a quasi-sacred site where reason and argument is supposed to dominate and advertising is often seen in popular imagination as a usurper of reason. Tragic events in the United States, Scotland and, most recently, in Beslan in Russia where children are killed in school have an added resonance as they occur in a place with these sacred connotations and have become sacred events.

Psychological approaches

The last approach I would advocate for obvious reasons as that is my own background. But I want to make a plea for an intelligent use of psychological theory and a request that developmental psychologists take the opportunity to test out theoretical perspectives using this rarely explored area of everyday child behaviour, as well as importing psychological theory into the debate on advertising to children. The example of how the child's awareness of how celebrity endorsement works could tell us a lot about children's understanding of acting and in general when and where 'not doing what you really feel' is appropriate. Similarly we need to explore the different streams of development when investigating the child's understanding of the intent behind advertising. Knowing that an ad is a symbolic representation of reality should be related to mainstream developmental work on the fantasy-reality distinction and knowing that someone is the 'author' of the advertisement with an interest in getting the recipient to do something must be related to 'theory-of-mind' research. Too frequently we read descriptions of some developmental sequence in the child's understanding of advertising with a passing reference to a textbook on Piaget added as an afterthought. There are many more theorists than Piaget (see John, 1999) and many more local theories in psychology that explore the development of specific skills that should act as theoretical support for an empirical study.

Let us also not forget that children and advertising can and should be contextualised in two already well-established fields – economic socialisation (see Webley et al., 2001) and consumer socialisation (John, 1999). There is already a good literature in both and we can only hope that other researchers will find a home in either.

References

Anon (1997); Walkers Crisps - Garymania! - how an already successful brand benefited from famous advertising, in G. Duckworth (Ed.), *Advertising Works 9*. Henley-on-Thames: NTC, Chapter 9, pp.203-230.

Barthes, R. (1973); *Mythologies*. St Albans: Paladin.

Belk, R. W., M. Wallendorf and J. F. Sherry (1989); The sacred and the profane in consumer behavior: theodicy on the odyssey. *Journal of Consumer Research, 16*, pp. 1-38.

Borzekowski, D. L. and T. N. Robinson (2001); The 30-second effect: an experiment revealing the impact of television commercials on food preferences of preschoolers. *Journal of the American Dietetic Association, 101*, pp. 42-46.

Cialdini, R. B. et al. (1976); Basking in reflected glory: Three (football) field studies. *Journal of Personality and Social Psychology, 34(3)*, pp. 366-375.

Clarke, J. (2002); The Internet according to kids. *International Journal of Advertising and Marketing to Children, 3(2)*, pp. 39-52.

Durkheim, É. (1913); *The Elementary Forms of the Religious Life.* Translated from French by Joseph Ward Swain. London: Unwin.

Flavell, J. H. (1963); *The Developmental Psychology of Jean Piaget.* Princeton, NJ: Van Nostrand.

Gamble, M. and N. Cotugna (1999); A quarter century of TV food advertising targeted at children. *American Journal of Health Behavior, 23(4)*, pp. 261-267.

Goldberg, M. E., G. J. Gorn and W. Gibson (1978); TV messages for snacks and breakfast foods: do they influence children's preferences? *Journal of ConsumerResearch, 5*, pp. 73-81.

Gorn, G. J. and M. E. Goldberg (1982); Behavioral evidence of the effects of televised food messages on children. *Journal of Consumer Research, 9*, pp. 200-205.

Halford, J. C. G., J. Gillespie, V. Brown, E. E. Pontin and M. Dovey (in press). Effects of television advertisements for foods on food consumption in children. *Appetite.*

Hastings, G., M. Stead, L. McDermott, A. Forsyth, A. M. MacKintosh et al. (2003); *Review of Research on the Effects of Food Promotion to Children. Final Report.* London: Food Standards Agency.

Huesmann, L. R. and M. M. Skoric (2003); Regulating media violence: why, how, and by whom?, in E. L. Palmer and B. M. Young (Eds.), *The Faces of Televisual Media: Teaching, Violence, Selling to Children.* Mahwah, NJ: Lawrence Erlbaum.

John, D. R. (1999); Consumer socialization of children: a retrospective look at twenty-five years of research. *Journal of Consumer Research, 26(3)*, pp. 183-213.

Jones, A. (2002); Wireless marketing: the linking value of text messaging. *International Journal of Advertising and Marketing to Children, 3(2),* pp. 39-44.

Kasser, T., R. M. Ryan, C. E. Couchman and K. M. Sheldon (2004); Materialistic values: Their causes and consequences, in T. Kasser and A.D Kanner (eds.), *Psychology and Consumer Culture.* (pp. 11-28). Washington, D.C.: American Psychological Association.

Kunkel, D. (2001); Children and television advertising, in D. G. Singer and J. L. Singer (Eds.), *The Handbook of Children and Media* (pp. 375-393). Thousand Oaks, CA: Sage.

Kunkel, D., B. L. Wilcox, J. Cantor, E. Palmer, S. Linn and P. Dowrick (2004); *Report of the APA Task Force on Advertising and Children. Section: Psychological Issues in the Increasing Commercialization of Childhood.* Washington DC: American Psychological Association.

Levi-Strauss, C. (1970); *The raw and the cooked.* Translated from the French 'le cru et le cuit' by John and Doreen Weightman. London: Cape.

Levin, D. E. and S. Linn (2004); The commercialization of childhood: understanding the problem and finding solutions, in T. Kasser and A.D Kanner (eds.), *Psychology and Consumer Culture.* (pp. 213-232). Washington, D.C.: American Psychological Association.

Palmer, E., J. Cantor, P. Dowrick, D. Kunkel, S. Linn and B. L. Wilcox (2004); *Psychological Implications of Commercialism in the Schools.* Washington DC: American Psychological Association.

Powell, J. and G. Wicken (2002); US kids and British children – identical or incomparable? *International Journal of Advertising and Marketing to Children, 3(3),* pp. 33-40.

Siegel, D. L., T. J. Coffey and G. Livingston (2001); *The Great Tween Buying Machine: Marketing to Today's Tweens.* Ithaca, NY: Paramount Market.

Scott, Sir W. (1806); *Marmion.* [Canto 6, st. 17].

Webley, P., C. B. Burgoyne, S. E. G. Lea, and B. M. Young (2001); *The Economic Psychology of Everyday Life*. Hove, UK: Psychology Press.

Williamson, J. (1978); *Decoding Advertisements: Ideology and Meaning in Advertising*. London: Marion Boyars.

World Health Organization (2000); *Obesity: Preventing and Managing the Global Epidemic*. Geneva: WHO Technical Report Series 894.

World Health Organization (2003); *Diet, Nutrition and the Prevention of Chronic Diseases*. Geneva: WHO Technical Report Series 916.

Young, B. M. (1990); *Television Advertising and Children*. Oxford: Oxford University Press.

Young, B. M. (2002); The child's understanding of the intent behind advertising: a personal story, in F. Hansen, J. Rasmussen, A. Martensen, and B. Tufte (Eds.), *Children - Consumption, Advertising and Media*. Frederiksberg DK: Samfundslitteratur, pp.181-202.

Young, B. M. (2004); *Does advertising to children make them fat? A sceptical gaze at irreconcilable differences.* Invited paper presented to a seminar organised by the ESRC and AHRB Cultures of Consumption Research Programme and held at the Royal Society on 19 February 2004.

Young, B. M., P. Webley, M. Hetherington and S. Zeedyk (1996); *The Role of Television Advertising in Children's Food Choice*. Report to the Ministry of Agriculture, Fisheries and Food (MAFF).

6

Children's and Adolescents' Use of the Internet – with Focus on Tweens

BIRGITTE TUFTE AND
JEANETTE RASMUSSEN

No matter where they live, Denmark, Spain, the USA, wherever, young people turn to the new media and communications culture with the same curiosity, enthusiasm and will to master the technology. The culture of children and young people is truly global when it comes to the media, and — given access — we find by and large the same patterns among young people the world over.

From at least this one point of view, the picture is relatively uniform. However, there are also a great number of nuances based on geography and economics as well as differences depending on whether the child lives in a country rich in media and having a high level of media and communications technology - or perhaps the opposite. There are social differences as well, based on the family's level of education and income, there are age-based differences, and, not least, there are differences between how boys and girls, respectively, use the media they have access to.

What is the Internet?

The Internet is a global high-speed network consisting of a vast number of computer networks linked around the world. The explosion of the Internet has occurred during the last decade all over the world.

As a matter of fact, the Internet has been available since the early 1960s, when it was developed for military purposes. However, it was not until the 1990s, when a new generation of software – the World Wide Web (WWW) browsers – was developed, that the Internet became widespread. The Internet delivers an enormous amount of information, which according to the American researchers (Strasburger and Wilson, 2002) could be described as follows:

- E-mail for electronic communication. Many would agree that this is certainly one of the most popular forms of communication in today's society. Even this simple and everyday form of technology has changed in recent years, with the ability to send voice, video and other forms of attachments around the world almost instantaneously.
- Bulletin board systems for posting information on almost any topic you could imagine.
- Chat groups that can be used for real-time conversations. For many adolescents, it is the global equivalent of a 'free' conference call. However, unlike the traditional conference call, you can choose your topic, person and time in any manner you desire.
- The World Wide Web, which combines visuals/sound/text in a manner that allows linkages across many sites that are related to a particular topic. These topics can obviously be those related to sex, violence, drugs, or any other content for which we have concerns.

Strasburger and Wilson, 2002: p. 304

International research

Media play an important role in the daily life of children all over the world, although there are differences depending on where the children live. The Internet is the newest member of the global family of media technology. Compared to other media, the Internet is highly interactive. Unlike traditional media, the Internet allows children and adolescents access to different kinds of content, and a specific characteristic is that this can be done in privacy, with little knowledge of the child's parents. In the USA, access to and use of the Internet is growing rapidly. A survey from 1999 of teenagers' use of the Internet reveals that 82% use the Internet. The percentage of American teenagers using the Internet is probably much higher today. The same survey says that 62% of teenagers know little or nothing about the websites they visit (Strasburger and Wilson, 2002: pp. 302-303). The survey also indicates that the most influential sources of information for teenagers in making decisions are media, meaning that children and adolescents receive far more information from media than from parents and schools. This phenomenon has been called 'the parallel school of media', which means that children and adolescents daily spend several hours on media culture through which they learn a lot of things that are not taught at school (Tufte, 1995).

In the following, we shall present some selected European findings regarding the Internet showing children and adolescents' use of the Internet, with focus on the rapid growth in the use of the Internet.

In Germany, a survey was carried out in 1998 showing that less than 1% of all children aged 6-13 used the Internet, and another survey carried out in 1997 regarding children and young people between the age of 12 and 17 showed that the largest section of child and adolescent users were aged 14-16. However, they did not use it frequently; only half of the 'on-liners' were regularly on the Internet. It was found that children mostly use the Internet for sending electronic messages (e-mails), for listening to sound and video files, and for chatting and playing on the Net (Gehle, 1999).

In conclusion of German children's use of the Internet in 1998, the following was stated:

> 'Online media such as the Internet harbour tremendous opportunities and can enrich children's everyday media use. Does this mean serious competition for the classical media such as television, radio and video games? At the moment, the Internet – at least in Germany – is (still) too chaotic, expensive and its contents too imperfect. But the success of services such as the Kindernetz of the Südwestrundfunk proves that there are quite a few children out there who make use of the new medium to satisfy their own highway. The role that the Internet plays now and will play in the future in the kids' media programme is still the subject of considerable speculation in Germany.'
>
> (Gehle, 1999)

A French study from 2001 (Bevort and Bréda, 2001) shows that 28% of young French people used the Internet at that time and that 30% of them had only used it once or twice. The study compared use at home and at school. It turned out that at home the Internet was used for entertainment purposes, whereas it was mainly used for schoolwork in school.

The report distinguishes two groups of users:

- Light users or those who do not use the Internet at all (mainly below the age of 15 years – and girls).
- Heavy users, who are between 15 and 17 years of age – and boys.

Bevort and Bréda, 2001: pp. 13-14

A comparative study among 12 European countries (Livingstone and Bovill, 2001) shows that there are rather large differences among the countries of Europe. Countries like Spain, Italy and France have a strong focus on national television and relatively low figures in new media technologies (including the computer and Internet access). The second group is made up of Germany, Switzerland, Belgium and Israel; all countries with a multi-channel environment and moderate use of new technologies. The UK is treated as a group on its own because – contrary to the pattern observed elsewhere – it combines a heavy orientation towards television with rather high figures for new technologies. The fourth group consists of the Nordic countries and the Netherlands; all countries that are seen as the pioneers in new media technologies (Livingstone and Bovill, 2001: p. 27).

A very recent UK study regarding 9-19 year-olds' use of the Internet (Livingstone, Bober and Helsper, 2004) has focussed on the online participation and examined children and young people's use of the Internet for:
- Communicating
- Peer-to-peer connection
- Seeking information
- Interactivity
- Webpage/content creation
- Visiting websites, civic and political websites

The study shows that

> 'some ways of interacting with websites (completing quizzes, sending emails) are fairly common – perhaps because they are already familiar practices in other media…But others are much less common, and this too may be because young people are not used to receiving and responding to requests to vote, offer advice, sign a petition, and so forth, in their everyday (offline) lives…'
>
> Ibid: p. 16

The survey also shows that 'boys, middle class and older teens have higher levels of internet self-efficacy, stay online longer per day and have been using the internet for longer … In other words, it appears that online interactivity and, particularly, online creativity can be encouraged through the very experience of using the internet …' (Livingstone, Bober and Helsper, 2004: p. 16.)

Danish findings show that there is a great deal of media equipment in children's own rooms. This is shown by Kirsten Drotner, who has been the Danish partner in the above-mentioned comparative European study. Her survey covers 6-16 year-olds (Drotner, 2001) and shows that at that time 60% had a TV in their own room, and although they also use the computer, it is a fact that television is the most used medium with 2½ hours per day on average. As has already been mentioned, various studies show that there are gender differences in the use of media. Drotner says that the gender differences in media use is very striking and goes beyond age and social background. This is especially true for computer games where 9-16 year-old boys spend four times as long on games as girls, whereas girls to a higher extent use computers for schoolwork. When it comes to the Internet, boys and girls use it for different purposes. Girls mostly use the Internet for surfing, chat and email, whereas boys use it for looking for information, producing websites and downloading software. Similar trends can be seen in a survey made by the Swedish media researcher Cecilia von Feilitzen of 15-24 year-olds' use of the Internet:

> 'Both boys and girls were of the opinion that television was the most important medium for entertainment/pleasure. As to knowledge and information, boys gave priority to the Internet in the first place and television in the second. The girls chose books first and television second.'
>
> Feilitzen, 2002: p. 108

The same trend can be seen in Table 6:1: Gender differences in media consumption for the 8-12 year-olds. The figure shows that both boys and girls spend the same amount of time watching TV on weekdays, but differ on other medias. Boys spend more time on computer games, play-station, the Internet and cartoons than girls, whereas girls spend most of their time on listening to radio and reading books and magazines.

Table 6:1. 8-12 year-olds' media consumption

Average no of minutes - Weekdays	Boys	Girls
Radio	11	20
TV	98	94
Video	26	25
The Internet	25	17
Computer games	56	27
Play-station	43	7
Books	24	33
Cartoons	24	20
Magazines	5	10

Source: TNS-Gallup's children and youth index 2003.

Tweens

As children and young people increasingly have their own money and influence the family's consumption, the interest of companies and advertisers in them is growing, and new and more sophisticated methods are being developed with a view to reaching this segment, especially the so-called tweens.

What is the definition of 'tweens'?

It is a group of 'in betweens', i.e. between childhood and adolescence. However, there remains some disagreement on a precise definition of age.

According to (Lindstrøm, 2003), the term tweens covers children in pre-adolescence until the age of 14 (i.e. 8-14 years of age). Our immediate reaction to this categorization is that all studies show that there is a great difference between being 8 years old and 14 years old.

(Siegel, Coffey and Livingstone, 2001) state that in marketing research tweens are generally regarded as the 8-12 age group, but there are also some who view 7-14 year-olds or 10-16 year-olds as tweens. Siegel et al. believe that it would be relevant to operate with the age group 8-12 year-olds as tweens and then possibly further distinguish between younger and older tweens, i.e. 8-10 year-olds and 11-12 year-olds.

With the commercialization and globalization of media, lifestyle, fashion and music, mobile phones and media culture are now subject to the principle of the lowest international common denominator, which means that the same 'brands' feature all over the industrialized world. All over the western world, children and young people wear the same jeans, eat the same burgers and pizzas, eat the same breakfasts, watch the same films on TV, video and DVD, listen to the same music and keep the same mobile phone in their pockets. And the velocity of circulation of what is 'cool' right here and now is becoming increasingly quicker – and is manifested globally in a very short time. The Internet is one such example of the fast technological development.

Whereas only 8% of Danish families had access to the Internet in 1997, the percentage in 2003 was 68%. And a close look at families with children reveals that 86% of these had Internet access in 2003. The tendency is more or less the same in other Nordic countries. However, this does not mean that it is safe to conclude that all children and young people in the entire world communicate via the Internet. The global differences are huge: only 27% of the world's population live in northern Europe and Canada, while 65% of the total number of Internet users live in northern Europe and Canada. In other words, we have a common transgressing media and consumption culture on the one hand, where children and young people are keeping up, and on the other hand, we can also see a polarization between those who are 'connected' via access to technology and those who do not have the same possibilities.

In our part of the world, however, it is a fact that children and young people are extremely quick to acquire new technology. They use the media simultaneously, are able to relate to multiple media at the same time, and maintain contact with each other – especially via the mobile phone, primarily communicating through instant (text) messaging. They sleep with the mobile phone on their pillow. The last thing they do before they sleep is turn off the mobile, and the first thing they do when they wake up is turn it on.

Two girls aged 10 and 11 years, respectively, recently said in an interview that they felt the new mobile phones, containing an incredible amount of possibilities, had been developed for their age group because *the grown-ups don't know how to use them.*

In other words, they are very conscious that they are keeping up with technology, more so than many adults. If one talks to schoolteachers, they are not always particularly impressed with the children's competence level, for instance in relation to the Internet.

Many teachers feel the children lack a deeper knowledge, among other things, about the Internet; a knowledge that transcends the 'clicking-capabilities' the children possess, a knowledge of relevant information searches, and a knowledge of rules and rights in relation to, for example, e-commerce, advertising on the Internet, etc. The need for children to have such knowledge is continuously growing with the increasing commercialization of the Internet.

One such example is a pilot study that PhD student Jeanette Rasmussen and I carried out in the spring of 2003 in three 4th grade classes. We asked 10-11 year-old children to write down the websites they knew and often visited. The result was 42 websites, most of which were commercial, such us Cartoon Network, Disney, and many of them not created for their age group.

Tweens' use of the Internet

'A new media landscape and a new media order are emerging. Media cultures are changing, in both the public and the private sphere …The volume of information conveyed via new media technologies continues to expand, while the distinctions betweens computers, television, radio, the press, books, and telephony gradually dissolve…Viewed in the longer term, new media technology and the changes we note in the media order have a profound influence on the conditions and cultures of children and young people. For many children in the world today, culture is something they partake of via electronic media.'

Carlsson, Nordicom 2000

In the news we constantly hear how advanced children are with computers and the Internet – far more than their parents. But what do we know about the Internet use of Danish tweens - the generation that was born with the computer? The following findings show the development of tweens' (8-12 year-olds) Internet use over a four-year period from 2000 to 2003. The data is from TNS-Gallup's annual children and youth media index, where around 2,800 interviews were carried out each year with children aged 5 to 18 years.

In 2003, almost all tweens (97.8 %) had a computer at home and also used it (96.9%). To relate the use of the Internet to other forms of use, it is interesting to look at *where* and *for what* purpose the children use the computer. As Table 6:2 shows, the most popular places to use the computer for the 8-12 year-olds has not changed over the four-year period. At home (96.9%) is still the most popular place, then in school (76.2%), with friends (52.7%), followed by the library (21.1%) and finally youth clubs (21.0%). What is also interesting is that the level of use in the different locations has more or less remained at the same level. Places where the Internet is used are the same as the locations for the computer.

Table 6:2. Places where the 8-12 year-olds use the computer

	2000	**2001**	**2002**	**2003**
At home	89.2	89.0	91.4	96.9
In school	73.9	73.4	70.1	76.2
With friends	48.4	51.4	43.6	52.7
The library	21.4	19.0	18.1	21.1
Youth clubs	10.1	10.5	9.7	21.0

Source: TNS-Gallup's children and youth media index 2000-2003

The computer is primarily used for playing games. In 2003, 93.3% used it for games, and the survey shows that there is a majority of boys using the computer for games. The Internet is the second most used activity on the computer, and this activity increased from 43.3% in 2000 to 55.6% in 2003. However, the computer is also used for schoolwork (43.4%) and for play and learning programmes (35.8%).

Table 6:3. Activities which the 8-12 year-olds use the computer for

	2000	**2001**	**2002**	**2003**
Games	90.2	88.6	91.1	93.3
Internet	43.3	47.5	43.8	55.6
Schoolwork	41.8	40.0	37.7	43.4
Play and learning programmes	33.3	34.7	35.6	35.8

Source: TNS-Gallup's children and youth media index 2000-2003

What does the data show about the 8-12 year-old's use of the Internet? What has highest priority? First and foremost, they play games – 61.2% in 2003. Secondly, they surf for particular websites (49.1%), although unfortunately the data does not tell us what kind of websites they visit. It is mainly friends that tell them about the different websites they find interesting (55.9% in 2003) and then it is their own exploring (40.8%). Furthermore, 17.5% indicated that they hear about websites from siblings, 18.3% reported that they learn about websites from commercials, and, finally, 16.7% stated they obtain their information from their parents.

Thirdly, they use the Internet to search for information for schoolwork (43.4%), which increased from 41.8% in 2000. This can probably be related to the government's focus on providing primary and secondary schools with more computers and that using the Internet is part of the curriculum.

Fourthly, they e-mail (36.2%) and chat over the Internet (24.1%). The Internet is also increasingly being used by the tween group to download a range of things from the Internet, but only among a minority of the total users. For example, on a scale from daily or almost daily to 1-5 times half-yearly, approximately 8% downloaded music from the Internet in 2003, approx. 9% downloaded programmes/files, approx. 15% downloaded pictures and approx. 4% downloaded wallpaper/screensavers. There is a legal aspect to the downloading of files and music, which both children and adolescents are aware of, but do not want to discuss:

> Interviewer: 'You download from the Net – can you do it with the computer you have down there?'
> Boy: 'Yes – it is very slow, so I do it mostly at one of my friend's places.'
> Interviewer: 'How long does it take to download?'
> Boy: 'It depends on the Internet connection.'
> Interviewer: 'What about this?'
> Boy: 'I don't know, maybe 20 minutes or so.'
> Interviewer: 'It really depends on how big the computer is?'
> Boy: 'And it also depends on where you download to. For example if it is another person that has it on his computer.'
> Interviewer: But is that legal?'
> Boy: 'Some are ok'[1].

---

[1] Interview with 15-year-old boy.

As mentioned, the Internet is increasingly being used by the children in school. However, it seems that some of the children do not trust all the information they receive and thus prefer books. In this respect, as already mentioned, there is a gender difference; girls are more oriented towards books, whereas boys often prefer the Internet.

> '...When we had to prepare a project, we were told that we shouldn't trust the Internet 100%. We were also to contact people that knew something about it... I have found a lot of information, including some that was false. I really don't trust the Internet. In my e-mail I get newsletters where I can win a trip or get a trip for a small amount of money –I don't trust that. I feel like it is some kind of scam.'
> Interviewer: 'Don't you think it is problematic when you prepare projects to go on the Internet to get information?'
> Girl: 'It is, but I almost never do; only if I need some specific information. Otherwise, I find some people and interview them or get books about it.'
> Interviewer: 'Have you bought anything over the Internet?'
> Girl: 'No. I am too afraid.'[2]

The development from 2000-2003 shows
- A steady but high percentage of children using the Internet
- Gender differences in the use of the Internet (especially in relation to games and chat)
- Downloading from the Internet is increasing.

Concerns about the Internet

Often parents, teachers and others express concern regarding children and young people's use of the Internet. The way children use the media and whether there are rules or not in relation to new media very much depends on the attitude of the family, and here families are different. In a 2½-year study examining media use in the family, four categories of families were observed:

- **The relaxed,** where children and adults are allowed to use media as they please. No direct rules of conduct within the

---

[2] Interview with 12-year-old girl.

family. The media do not disturb family life, but are viewed as 'natural' and an integral part of family life.

- **The caring/protective,** where there are rules guiding the media use as a form of protection and to facilitate everyday family life. The media development should not dictate everyday family life, which is why media use must be controlled.
- **The democratic/pluralistic,** where media use is up for discussion and debate, but where there is no direct set of rules or agreement. On the contrary, the parents try to convince their children by arguing their point, i.e. 'common sense' rules.
- **The unifying,** where the family union and 'the concept of us' are important. In this perspective, media use is not viewed as particularly important, but rules for media use are decided for the family as a unity if necessary. The parents support their children's media use as long as it does not 'get out of hand'.

Christensen and Tufte, 2001

The attitudes and concerns of the families very much focus on the time spent on media and on the violence in media. The fact that media globally are becoming commercialized during these years does not seem to worry the parents so much. On this perspective, Sonja Livingstone comments:

'Less attention has been paid to the commercial 'dangers' of the internet, though there is growing criticism over the ways in which children's rights to privacy may be violated by online advertising and unfair or deceptive practices …However, little research has examined the user's perspective in order to discover how teens respond to such sites (i.e. commercial websites), and whether they can recognize and/or distance themselves from commercial approaches.'

Livingstone, 2003

Tweens – between media and consumption

As mentioned above, the tweens group has in recent years been eliciting and increasing interest, whereas some years ago teenagers were the objects of interest for the business world as researchers.

Currently, interest is particularly keen among companies, advertisers and media, whereas research interest towards this middle-group has been relatively small. This is partly the basis for the research project 'Tweens – between media and consumption – A study of 10-12 year-old children's use of media, focussing on the interplay between different media – in relation to children's identity formation and socialisation as consumers.'

The project, theoretically and methodologically, is partly inspired by Sonja Livingstone, who emphasizes that what is needed are:

- Studies focussing on children's own interests – children as active interpreters - (the significance of peer communication, school, networks, family)
- Studies combining content and reception analysis
- Longitudinal studies

The two-year project aims to examine the extent to which the media play a role for the consumer behaviour of 10-12 year-old children in relation to other socialization factors, such as family, school and friends.

As already mentioned, there has in recent times been a great interest in children's consumer behaviour, whereas previously media behaviour and preferences were in focus. As stated, the interest emanates from the business world and advertisers, but also from teachers, parents and politicians, etc., who are guided by other interests than companies and advertisers. Often, however, the public discourse on children, media and consumption has focussed very narrowly on whether children are either competent or vulnerable in relation to media and consumption. Hopefully, this ongoing project will be able to contribute with more nuanced perspectives on this issue.

The basis for the project is:

- That there has presently been a convergence within the media-technological area.
- That children use media convergently, i.e. they communicate across technologies.
- That the selected group – the 10-12 year-olds, the so-called tweens – is a group whose media and consumer behaviour has not been examined on a larger scale.
- That a continuously growing internationalization and commercialization of the media is taking place in conjunction with an increasing number of messages targeted at tweens.

- That Danish companies are increasingly orientating themselves towards tweens as a consumer group.

The project consists of a common, general project and three subprojects with the following titles:
1. 10-12 year-old children's converging use of media – with special focus on the Internet.
2. The media's significance for 10-12 year-olds' identity and socialization as consumers.
3. 10-12 year-old children's experience and understanding of TV advertising.

Danish as well as international research indicates that the media play a significant role in the consumer socialization of children, just as a number of research results, primarily based on quantitative data, has documented that children have a comparatively large amount of money at their disposal and that to a large extent they influence the family's consumption.

Quantitative as well as qualitative research elucidating the extent to which the different media interact in the consumer socialization of older children are, however, lacking, as are reception analyses of children's own understanding and attitudes to media and consumption. The aim and expectations regarding the project 'Tweens – between media and consumption' is to examine these problems and find an answer to them.

Theoretically, the project is based on theory from media research as well as consumer research, which so far have represented two distinct areas. We intend to combine relevant parts of these two different research traditions in relation to the project's problem area.

Presently, in December 2004, data from a quantitative questionnaire survey is being processed, with the data coming from responses given by 4th, 5th and 6th grade pupils at four schools. The pupils were also asked to make drawings of their room and to write a Christmas wishlist. Consequently, having just finished the collection of data in the four schools, we are in the first phase of analysis.

On the basis of the analysis and interpretation of the 'texts', i.e. the questionnaires, the drawings and the Christmas present wishes, some of the tweens will be selected for in-depth interviews in the spring of 2005. The project is due to be completed at the beginning of 2006.

References

Bevort, Évelyne and Isabelle Bréda (2001); *Les jeunes et Internet*. Ministére De L'education National: CLEMI.

Buckingham, David (2002); The Electronic Generation? Children and New Media, in L. A. Lievrouw and Sonia Livingstone (ed.), *The Handbook of New Media*. London: SAGE Publications.

Carlsson, Ulla (2000); Introduction, in Feilitzen, C. v. and U. Carlsson, *Children in the New Media Landscape*. Göteborg. The UNESCO International Clearinghouse on Children and Violence on the Screen at Nordicom.

Christensen, Ole and Birgitte Tufte (2001); *Familier i forandring – hverdag og medier i danske familier*. Copenhagen: Akademisk Forlag.

Drotner, Kirsten (2001); *Medier for fremtiden: børn og unge og det nye medielandskab*. Copenhagen: Høst and Søn.

Feilitzen, Cecilia von (2002); Times are changing and youth with them on young people's media use in Sweden, in Hansen et al. (ed.), *Children – Consumption, Advertising and Media*. Samfundslitteratur, Copenhagen.

Frønes, I. and R. Brusdal (2000); *På sporet av den ny tid – kulturelle varsler for en nær fremtid*. Bergen: Fagbokforlaget.

Gehle, Tobias (1999); Children on the Internet, in Paul Löhr and Mamfred Meyer, *Children, Television and the New Media*. Munich: University of Luton Press, pp. 134-145.

Halling, J. and B. Tufte (2002); *The Gender Perspective – In Relation to Children as Consumers*. Research Paper no. 15. Copenhagen Business School: Department of Marketing

Hansen, Flemming et al. (2002); *Børns opvækst som forbrugere*. Copenhagen: Samfundslitteratur.

Hansen, Flemming et al. (2002); *Children – Consumption, Advertising and Media*. Copenhagen: Samfundslitteratur.

Kenway, J. and E. Bullen (2001/2003); *Consuming Children.* Maidenhead, Philadelphia: Open Univeristy Press.

Kjørstad, Ingrid (2000); *Barn og internet*-reklame. Lysaker: SIFO.

Lindstrøm, M. (2003); *Brandchild.* Copenhagen: Forlaget Markedsføring.

Livingstone Sonia (2003); "Children's use of the Internet: reflections on the emerging research agenda, in N. Jankowski et al. (ed.), *New Media and Soci*ety, vol. 5(2), ed. 1. London: Thousand Oaks, CA and New Delhi: Sage Publications, pp. 147-167.

Livingstone, Sonia and Moira Bovill (2001); *Children and· Their Changing Media Environment. A European Comparative* Study. London: Lawrence Erlbaum Associates, Publishers.

Livingstone, Sonia et al. (2004); *Active participation or just more information.* A research report from the UK Children Go Online project.

Lynne, A. (2000); *Nyansenes makt – en studie av ungdom, identitet og klær.* Oslo: SIFO.

Montgomery, Kathryn (2001); The New On-Line Children's Consumer Culture, in Dorothy and Jerome Singer (ed.), *Handbook of Children and the Media.* London: Sage publications, pp. 635-50.

Rogers, Everett M. (1995); *Diffusion of Innovations, vol.4.* New York: Free Press.

Siegel, D.L., T. J. Coffey and G. Livingston (2001); *The Great Tween Buying Machine.* Ithaca, New York: Paramount Market Publishing, Inc.

Storm Mathisen, A. (1998); *Kjøpepress ... hva er det for noe ?* Arbejdsrapport nr. 4. Oslo: SIFO (Statens institutt for forbruksforskning).

Strasburger, Victor C. and Barbara J. Wilson (2002); *Children, Adolescents, and the Media.* California: Sage Publications.

Tapscott, Don (1998); *Growing Up Digital – The Rise of the Net Generation*. New York: McGraw-Hill.

Tufte, Birgitte (1995); *Medier og skole*. Copenhagen: Akademisk Forlag.

Tufte, Birgitte (2003); *Girls in the New Media landscape*. In Nordicom Review, Gothenburg. (in press).

Turkle, Sherry (1995); *Life on the Screen: Identity in the Age of the Internet*. New York: Simon and Schuster.

Zinckernagel, Peter (2003); *Children's use of digital media in and outside school*. Lecture on a conference on Children and IT, Copenhagen.

7

The Invention of the Child Consumer:
What is at Stake for Marketing Practice and Research?

VALÉRIE-INÉS DE LA VILLE

Introduction: The child as a target for marketing management

In this chapter, we aim at giving a rapid overview of the social conditions that lead to the emergence of a new category for managerial action in our Western post-modern societies: the child as a consumer.

In the first part, we very roughly lay emphasis on two main evolutions that seem to have smoothly prepared the ground for a strong connection between children and consumption:
- The contemporary focus on childhood in our societies, witnessed through several institutional advances and which has led to a reconsideration of children's abilities.
- The mundane nature of consumption practices that pervade extensively into the various realms of social relationships.

Through their combination, these changes have opened the possibility of enacting the child as a full consumer in our contemporary world. Consequently, this social construction has strengthened the emergence of children-oriented markets and reinforced the need to adapt conventional marketing techniques to deal with this promising, although difficult, commercial target.

In the second part, we attempt at characterizing the field of children's consumerism as a complex open system, which is partly shaped and transformed by managerial action. When aiming at children as consumers, marketing practice has to face a bundle of intermingled dimensions, which increase uncertainty as far as brand loyalty and profitability are concerned. Moreover, children-oriented commercial activities appear to constitute a highly ambiguous and controversial field upon which several institutions fiercely confront their ideological standpoints. On such a sensitive topic, forms of resistance to the ideology associated to mass consumption emerge with unusual intensity, thus ending in a deep reappraisal of both marketing managers' responsibility and the long-term contribution of marketing itself as a social institution.

Our concluding remarks call for a transformative agenda in marketing research in order to avoid reducing the child to a mere *'ego consumans'* (Baudrillard, 1970: p. 121) and to promote socially responsible research practices and ethically embedded theoretical frameworks likely to contribute to a meaningful renovation of the marketing discipline as a whole.

Part I -
The progressive connection of children with consumption

Enacting children as actors in consumption practices

The actual meaning of the notion of childhood depends strongly on other contextual factors that co-exist at a precise time of history within a given society. The rising importance of the child within our contemporary world appears as a social construction activated by several sociological trends and the diffusion of new scientific knowledge divulged by psychologists.

Reconsidering the child: agency and creativity:
From a sociological standpoint, the child appears to be constructed as a project that defines and legitimizes the family nucleus. In contrast with previous social practices, the contemporary focus on the child can be considered as the building block of family relationships. Therefore, family is no more conceived of as a long-lasting and unquestionable institution but has become a kind of temporary social arrangement in order to welcome and raise children. In addition, the model of parent-child relationships is transformed from an authoritarian model centred on the *'pater familias'* into a more egalitarian way of handling intra-family relationships. Children are invited by their parents to take part in certain decisions and to give their own opinions on the social

activities that the family nucleus should be involved in, such as holidays, sports and leisure (Singly, 1996; Singly et al., 2004).

From a psychological standpoint, several advances have led to an acknowledgement of the child as a full person (Dolto, 1985). Several works have underlined that long-lasting trauma undergone by adults often have their origin in early childhood. Other works have laid special emphasis on the importance of taking into account the child's own wishes and avoiding creating situations likely to provoke severe frustrations and difficulties in socialization. This psychological vulgate has been actively widespread through the media, through all the magazines aimed at parents, and through the explosion of websites dedicated to giving advice to parents on how to raise their children properly.

In a nutshell, the main consequences of these far too roughly sketched evolutions are threefold:

- *The recognition of children's agency*: The child is considered as a person and is able to make its own decisions. Parents are thus advised to ask for the child's opinion in some circumstances before making important or very ordinary decisions, like purchases. Some practices, which characterize children's behaviour, such as zapping TV programmes, the willingness to experiment with new products and the incapacity to achieve brand loyalty, can be analysed as proper decisions made by children aimed at exploring the social and cultural context in which they live.

- *The recognition of children's cultures*: Children are able to create their own social rules and to divert words and objects belonging to the realm of adulthood to generate their own socially shared meanings and cultures. Very often, children invent cultural practices that are inaccessible to adults and aimed at resisting adults' normative pressure. The heroes and celebrities they admire, the new forms of narratives they explore, the games and playing activities they are involved in, and the possibilities brought by the technologies they learn to use are all constitutive elements of children's culture, quite distant sometimes from their parents' culture (Buckingham, 2000).

- *The importance of children's socialization*: Birthday celebrations are a very emblematic form of children's socialization, where the convenient social rules to be followed are defined not only by parents but also by the children themselves. Children develop their own rituals and other meaningful socializing events that often take place in the schoolyard or in different playgrounds (Sirota, 1999).

The conjunction of these ideas that children a) have the capacity to decide their own activities, b) are quite creative in structuring their own cultures, and c) need to achieve a successful socialization, has prepared the ground for the emergence of a new category for managerial action in contemporary society: the child as a consumer.

Pragmatic evidence of the role children play in consumerism:
Several consultancy firms have recently presented strong evidence of the growing importance of children's consumerism in our contemporary society. Children are depicted as holding an increasing purchase power and an ever-growing influence on the household purchases, as well as having the capacity to transform the consumption habits of the household by introducing innovative products.

Direct and indirect purchasing power: In 2000, American children spent about USD 155 billion. However, this amount drastically increases when their savings are included (Siegel et al., 2002). In France, the consultancy firm Altavia Junium estimates that French children's annual purchasing power includes:
- EUR 33.10 billion of direct purchase (with their own money)
- EUR 2.85 billion for young people aged 11-17, without the possibility of formal employment
- EUR 8.38 billion for young people aged 18-20, some of whom are engaged in formal employment
- EUR 21.88 billion for young people aged 21-24, of whom 47.1% are engaged in formal employment (Le Bigot et al., 2004).

Discretionary spending: The amounts of money directly handled by children have dramatically increased in recent years. Indeed, grandparents play an important role through the money they give to their grandchildren, and the expenses they make for them are often an indirect help to their own children. The best way to develop consumption skills is to leave the child to experiment by itself. The dramatic rise in the amounts of pocket money given to children is an element of this educational perspective. In this context, children have the opportunity to make purchases outside parental control. They can often go to see movies with friends, buy small toys, buy magazines, buy clothes, eat in fast-food restaurants with their friends, buy snacks and junk food, play on-line in cybercafés for a few hours, etc.

Prescriptive power: Children's influence on family purchases is constantly increasing. According to a survey by the French polling institute IPSOS in 2003[1], some parents acknowledge that their young child influences sometimes up to 80% of their purchases in certain categories of products (e.g. food and clothes) As children aged 4-14 spend 2h33 daily watching TV[2], it is possible to calculate that they are exposed to 26,000 advertisements on average per year. Recent studies also demonstrate that babies are able to recognize logos from the age of 6 months and that brands are among the first words a young child pronounces. Thus, brands are part of the cultural background in which children develop their early cognitive and social skills.

The innovative behaviour of children: As far as consumption is concerned, children act as innovators. Through their prescriptive power, they manage to introduce new items in the household, such as cereals at breakfast, and they also contribute to transforming some consuming routines within the family. Children also appear to be experts - compared to adults – in the use of new technologies (mobile phones, satellite TV, consoles, Internet, video games, etc.) and they push their parents to consider the technical innovations offered by the market.

Beyond controversies about how realistic these figures can claim to be, consultancy firms have contributed to making children a kind of new 'Eldorado' that managerial action ought to conquer and colonize.

The mundane nature of children's consumerism

Within the household, consuming is a very ordinary and routinized social activity. Little by little, children are gradually involved in several consumption processes with their parents or grandparents, their siblings or peers, thus being naturally trained to become skilled consumers.

---

[1] IPSOS-Sofinco (2003), L'influence des enfants sur le budget familial – Etude européenne. http://www.ipsos.fr/CanalIpsos/articles/1109.asp?rubId=21

[2] Mediametrie (2004), Durée d'écoute par individu de la télévision, December.

Consumption: from rational decision-making to ordinary activity:
In the field of marketing, the study of young consumers' socialization has developed on the basis of the knowledge established thanks to the study of the adult consumer's buying behaviour. The adult consumer is characterized by his decisional autonomy, his logical skills to compare the attributes of products, his capacity to master the language to explain the reasons behind his choices and the relative stability of his preferences. The study of the child consumer has been organized by comparison with the adult and naturally resulted in underlining the cognitive, linguistic and behavioural limits of the child compared to the adult (La Ville, 2004). The restricted semantic field that the child masters does not enable it to explain its preferences precisely, these being based rather on a visual or oral memory or on emotional reactions. The child prioritizes the emotional register over pure logic to appreciate and compare the products, which reflects its preference for familiar brands (Hite et al. 1995). As a result, the reflexes of marketing managers with regard to persuasive communication techniques, brand recognition and enhancement of consumer loyalty must be suspended in the case of a child consumer.

To approach the meaning that consumer practices assume for the child, it seems necessary to achieve a shift in perspectives, and to move from buyer behaviour to detailed accounts of consumption practices (Ostergaard and Jantzen, 2000).

The study of consumption has emerged as in the mid-1980s, with a strong focus on the negative aspects of private consumption (Baudrillard, 1970). Post-modernist thought deeply transformed this emergent understanding of consumption by exploring the dreams, images and pleasures associated with consumer culture (Maffesoli, 1996). Nevertheless, this interpretation of the symbolic and communicative significance of consumption shed light on its spectacular side, while leaving in the shadow less flamboyant or visible practices:

> *'Too much emphasis has been placed upon:*
> - *Extraordinary rather than ordinary items*
> - *Conspicuous rather than inconspicuous consumption*
> - *Individual choice rather than contextual and collective constraint*
> - *Conscious, rational decision-making rather than routine, conventional and repetitive conduct*

> - *Decisions to purchase rather than practical contexts of appropriation and use*
> - *Commodified rather than other types of exchange considerations of personal identity rather than collective identification.'*

Gronow and Warde, 2001: p. 4.

This initial development of the field of consumption studies might explain why the role children play in consumption has hardly been considered for such a long while. Led in their explorations by the principle of consumer sovereignty, consumption studies were centred on adult meaning construction and symbolic communication (Bourdieu, 1984; Douglas, 1996) and did not consider children as skilled and reflexive enough consumers to master the meaning of the consumption practices in which they were involved. Unable to meet the requirements of such a consumer sovereignty principle – an autonomous capacity to decide by themselves the means for the satisfaction of their wants - children seem to have been disregarded in consumption studies for several decades.

'Considering that the mundane nature of consumption practices allows a reintegration of underestimated dimensions - like routines and ordinary products - and calls for a detailed account of some marginal actors' intervention in consumption practices, some room opened then to take into account the way children influence the household consumption habits and how they influence each other's preferences and satisfaction. In that perspective, we propose to regard child consumption as a mediated social activity (La Ville and Tartas, 2005) and not as a pure decision-making process, the expression of a structure of preferences or the result of a process of socialization. If each one of these dimensions is relevant by itself, the absence of controlled connections between them induces questionable forms of reductionism.

Consumption: a mediated and mediating joint activity:
We propose to call upon the concepts of '*joint activity*' and of '*cultural mediator*' suggested by (Jerome Bruner, 1990) and (Lev Vygotsky, 1933/1985) in order to study child consumption. Vygotsky brilliantly contended that children's ordinary activities are always mediated through cultural tools, such as language, symbols, techniques, signs and categories, and by an adult or a more experienced child.

The child does not enter the world of consumption alone: The entry into the consumer society constitutes a long training period during which the child passes from a situation of total dependence, in particular with respect to its parents, to the progressive construction of forms of autonomy to develop its own practices of consumption. Thus, child consumption constitutes an activity during which the child does not find itself on its own, but is supervised and guided by others to learn how to solve a certain number of conceptual and practical problems. Consequently, the relevant unit of analysis is certainly not the isolated child confronted with a problem to be dealt with, but rather the joint activity within an interaction 'child – adult', or of an interaction 'child - more experienced child' or of a small group, confronted with a problem (purchase decision, use of the object, etc.). Within this framework, the child is clearly integrated into a social body, which at the same time exceeds it, seeks it out and reassures it as it learns.

The child does not enter the world of consumption directly: According to Jerome Bruner, inter-subjectivity cannot be reduced to a one-to-one situation, as it includes the object on which mutual attention will be able to focus itself. This inter-subjectivity constitutes the foundation of the joint activity thanks to which the child discovers the world of objects under the guidance of the adult or a more experienced child. This perspective leads to the consideration that the other is always present in the activity of consumption as practised by a child and also to the perception of child consumption as a co-elaborated activity. Indeed, it is by engaging in a joint activity with a partner that the child gradually explores all the potential significance of the object being used.

As a mediated activity, consumption is also situated: The meaning of children's consumption is framed both by the normative demands of the family consumption style and the normative requirements of the peers' consumption styles. The child has to learn to deal with the conflictive requirements held by the different social groups it belongs to (Page and Ridgway, 2001). In doing so, it develops its rhetorical and negotiation skills to obtain satisfaction or sometimes it has to accept some frustration. But beyond these face-to-face relationships, children's consumerism is also enabled and constrained by wider social systems including:

- The institutionalized consumption arenas (e.g. distribution and retailing, regulatory requirements, admitted sales techniques,

142

sales on Internet, and cultural events like Christmas, Easter and Carnival festivities).

- The on-going innovativeness of the socio-technical system that allows new possibilities to design products aimed at children. For instance, 'smart toys' or interactive, cuddly toys like 'Furbies[3], by virtue of the fact that they mix electronics and traditional techniques, reflect in part the historical development of the toy industry and the new possibilities offered by technical innovation.

Figure 7:1

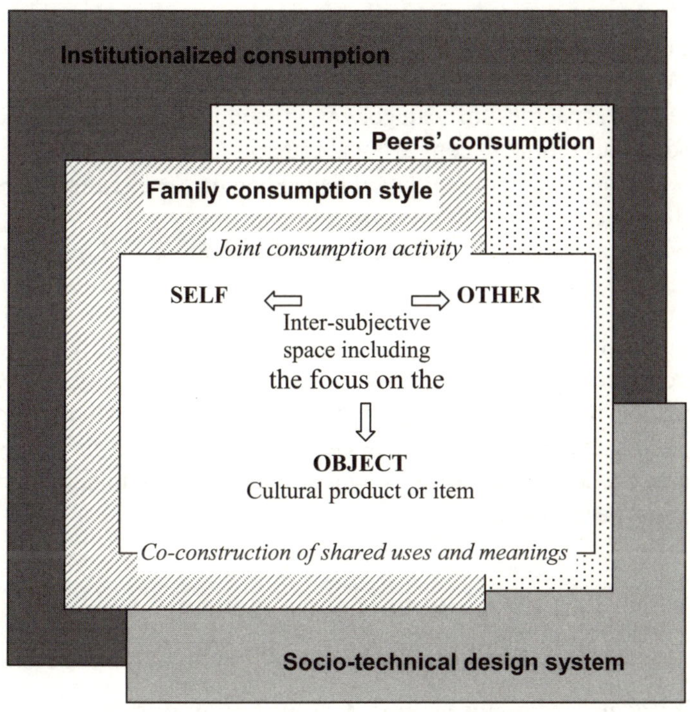

Child consumption as a mediated and also mediating social activity: If child consumption can be considered as a mediated activity – through the guidance of an adult or a more experienced child, through language, through packaging and advertising, etc. - it is extremely important to understand that it is also a mediating social activity. This

---

[3] A toy by HASBRO.

means that when participating in a consumption activity, the child learns many things far beyond consumption itself. When choosing a gift for a birthday party for instance, the child learns that different social rules have to be called on if the beneficiary is a boy or a girl, or an adult, etc. Moreover, when consuming or using an item, the child discovers and learns plenty of important notions concerning social life and its normative requirements. When using/consuming a product, the child develops its own skills by exerting its capacities on a concrete object. From this point of view, the child is an apprentice-consumer, who must gradually master a complex set of social skills, i.e:

- Learn linguistic expressions and a vocabulary directly attached to situations of consumption.
- Differentiate the particular situations of consumption and the values associated to them.
- Collect useful information concerning the product to be bought.
- Develop capacities of categorization and comparison of the products according to conventional criteria.
- Develop a capacity of regulation depending on the circumstances and products.
- Develop a socially acceptable use of the purchased product, object or service.

As a consequence, children's consumerism cannot be reduced to a mere purchase decision: educational and social dimensions are at the very heart of the long process allowing children to take part in consumption social practices; a characteristic that might explain why parents are so watchful when choosing a product or trying to help their child to resist peer pressure.

Part II - Children's consumerism: The new frontier of managerial practice?

Children's Consumerism: A complex open system

From a managerial standpoint, the field of children's consumerism can be conceptualized as a system of social practices which develops at the crossroads of five strongly intermingled complementary sub-systems (La Ville, 2004):

Five intertwined co-evolving sub-systems:
A relational system, which covers the relationships established with all the members of the family, especially with parents, siblings and grandparents, but also with persons in charge of raising the child, such as teachers and peers.

An institutional system, which includes the different institutions in charge of welcoming the child and providing it with all the necessary skills to successfully integrate in a given society. The institutional dimension refers to the notion of social role: at school, the child increases its knowledge, but it also learns to behave as a pupil; within its family, the child learns to differentiate the role and responsibilities reserved for parents and those reserved for children.

A plurimedia system, which encompasses all the media that the child learns to use in the course of its development. If television stands out as the preferred media of young kids, the latter learn very rapidly, for example, to use computers, to read magazines, to listen to the radio, to record music, to send e-mails, to send SMS on mobiles and to surf on the Internet.

A narrative system, which gathers together stories, fairy tales, narrations, fiction heroes, characters and other celebrities in real life, etc. that the child knows and recognizes. This narrative system offers concrete and symbolic markers to which the child refers when trying to explore the meaning of what it experiences, when expressing itself and when exercising its judgment capacity.

An economic system, which includes all the children-oriented markets, the different regulatory frames, and the different actors intervening in the dynamics of new product design process, distribution, marketing communication, etc. This system partly covers the socio-technical design system and the institutionalized consumption contexts previously mentioned. This system also includes consumer associations and all the protesters who strongly fight against capitalist ideology.

The field of children's consumerism can then be approached as a social construction to which several institutions contribute: consultants, industrials, governmental bodies, families, media, consumer associations, etc. As it is simultaneously embedded in all these sub-systems, managerial action aimed at selling and marketing products to children is a quite complex task.

It is undeniable, for instance, that managerial decisions have a direct impact on children's cultures. A worldwide success such as Pokémon not only commits children to new forms of play, but also becomes part of their cultural background, leading to a redefinition of playing. Henceforth, the launch of new products or toys has to take into account the transformation of playing modes achieved by the success of Pokémon (Tobin et al., 2004). The same happens in the video game industry: a blockbuster like The SIMS – 60% of players are girls - is bound to profoundly influence girl's future expectations concerning video games. Moreover, Mum and Dad are constantly losing ground in the ranking of persons that young children admire most and identify with. The marketing efforts to promote celebrities and cartoon characters lead them to become the main persons that children look up to. It is also obvious that managerial actions have a direct impact on children's way of socializing and lifestyles. The development of new forms of socialization – through TV programmes, video games and Internet - has smoothly led children to prefer virtual playgrounds and become more sedentary. Having fun with sports is nowadays synonymous with playing a game by Electronic Arts! (Kline, 2004) The roots of the phenomenon of 'Lolitas' – with its consubstantial magazines, cosmetics and fashion shops adapted to tween girls, etc. – can be partly found in active marketing campaigns aimed at girls aged from 8 to 12 years old (Russel and Tyler, 2004).

Managerial decision-making has to cope with complex trade-offs:
From a managerial standpoint, taking part in the field of children's consumerism and contributing to its long term evolution is a difficult endeavour. The trade-offs between the five sub-systems are so intense that they redesign the scope of activities that firms have to cover in order to play a significant part in children-oriented markets. We can sketch five major changes that are transforming managerial practice on these markets:

The need for a multidimensional innovation: If we examine the most appealing successes on children-oriented markets in the last ten years, we observe that they result from a multidimensional design. In order to market toys to young kids, it becomes imperative to simultaneously launch an animated series on TV. When launching a video game aimed at adolescents, it is necessary to anticipate cultural trends and actively engage in a competitive search for high potential character licences from the cinema or the publishing industries. Consequently, strategic awareness and vigilance have to focus on weak signals (Ansoff, 1984) likely to indicate the possible emergence of a consistent cultural world meaningful to children. But understanding the emerging cultural trends likely to shape children's lives is not easy at all, as they can disappear very quickly if competing worlds are more attractive.

Plurimedia marketing management: The product becomes only a part, a piece of a broader cultural context meaningful to children. Toys, video games, animated TV series and animated feature films are now strongly linked, as they contribute to creating a meaningful and consistent cultural world for kids. Consequently, marketing management cannot be reduced to communication and promotional efforts to launch the product. It has to build a complex set of relationships with partners from other industries to conceive and implement an actual strategic plan in order to exploit a property (a character or a product) in the long run through different media. The possibilities for greater diversity in entertainment activities offered to kids are therefore constrained by the pressure both to cast a wide promotional net over a mass audience with a single product and to consolidate brand identity through licensing agreements (Kline et al., 2003).

Enriching core competences: From a strategic standpoint, the main difficulty is to establish and sustain a network of complementary assets and idiosyncratic know-how in order to enrich core competences and enable a multidimensional design of a meaningful cultural world aimed at children. The multiple buyouts that have taken place in recent years – most of them leading to bitter failures – show how difficult it is to integrate different industrial traditions in order to meet children's expectations. Diversification is always a difficult managerial attempt, as the cultural distance between a producer of cultural goods (TV series or animated feature films) - who prioritizes artistic content, and a toy manufacturer - whose concerns are mainly industrial and mass market promotional techniques - might be sometimes insuperable.

Problems of rhythm and pace in decision-making: In some situations, a firm can originate the innovation and try to increase its long-term value. But in other circumstances, the company will have to behave as a follower and then its own evolution will depend on the rhythm and pace of innovation imposed by its partner. The example of the difficulties of LEGO in the last few years illustrates this phenomenon. Another difficulty is to be competent enough to understand the latest technical advances in different media – media convergence or not? - and to successfully bet on the best technology for the future. Another difficult stake consists in being able to adapt to the different standards imposed by different countries. To preserve its technical independence, China for instance is establishing its own standards in DVD, mobile phones, etc. Moreover, character licensing and its subsequent validation processes can seriously hinder global reactivity of the licensees and endanger the capacity of achieving an efficient merchandising.

Problems of scale in risk-taking: If the long-term exploitation of a cultural property is a key to achieving a successful and profitable strategy, then the best thing to do is to create and promote an original cultural world. Two French toy manufacturers – SMOBY, which creates a new product line 'Cotoons for young kids as well as BERCHET, which launches 'Les Amis de la Forêt' at the same age target - have chosen to promote simultaneously figurines and TV animated series. Because of the necessary extended promotional net to create brand awareness, the initial investments are drastically increased as well as the risks induced in case of failure. Moreover, when LEGO pays a high amount of royalties to obtain the licence for Harry Potter or Star Wars, it concentrates risk-taking on one or two expensive options, leaving other possibilities for new product design unexplored.

...Desperately searching for meaning

When a couple are expecting their first child, the search for meaning in consumerism is bound to change. When there is a child in a household, consumption habits change and new considerations are taken into account when choosing a product. Nowadays, it is not only a matter of nostalgic attitude that would lead parents to choose products emblematic of their own childhood, but it is also a far more profound evolution, as consumers are now quite experienced and able to go beyond marketing rhetoric to check important information in their own perspective. When buying products for their wanted child, parents are likely to start asking different questions about brands and products, such as:

- What is the quality of the ingredients included in that meal prepared for my child?
- Under which conditions is this toy or sportswear item aimed at children manufactured?
- What is the actual educational value of this expensive toy that is aimed at fostering the learning skills of my child?
- Is it appropriate to expose my child to violent entertainment programmes on TV or on video games?

- What kind of ecological choices are made by firms that proclaim they put the interests of children first?
- In what condition will we leave the planet to our children?

Children's consumerism: a privileged ground for resistance:
The field of children's consumerism constitutes indeed a privileged ground for ideological and legal battles aimed at challenging the foundations of the dominant order that capitalist society imposes on citizens.

Michel de Certeau's analysis of consumption (1988) is oriented towards the ordinary practices of consumers, who are defined as users of goods imposed on them by producers. Indeed, as an offer of products to consumers, production entails a logic of domination towards which consumers resist by developing inventive attitudes and practices. By mirroring consumption and reading, Michel de Certeau reveals the two sides of consumption: on the one side, consuming entails a form of acceptance of an imposed offer of goods, while on the other side, consumers are neither passive nor docile, experiencing freedom, creativity and pleasure – as readers do - in their consumption practices. In that perspective, meaningful practice is neither determined nor captured by the set of social rules in which it develops, but instead provokes a variety of hardly conscious, though crafty, tactics. Focusing on tactics sheds light on the creativity through which groups or individuals escape the 'nets of discipline' and resist the logic imposed upon them. Multiple tactics appear through a creative bricolage and reveal the extent to which ordinary intelligence is inseparable from everyday struggles and the pleasure they provide. As a consequence, studying the practice of consumption implies paying more attention to consumers' 'poaching ability' and the multiple ways through which, in their everyday activities, they understand, use and transform the dominant orders that are imposed on them.

Consumers also organize themselves in consumer associations which are very active and do not hesitate to sue for damages, misleading advertising campaigns or uncompetitive practices. Even though they are not fooled by their individual capacity to transform the system as a whole, consumers themselves engage in huge boycotts concerning products or brands (Klein, 2000). The idea that we live in a Risk Society that docile consumers have contributed to creating, also urges parents to change their individual behaviours. An alternative press is now emerging whose announced objective is to educate consumers and help them defeat socially unacceptable marketing practices. A French survey institute[4] announced in July 2004 that 25% of French consumers behave as 'alter-consumers', i.e. reject brands, use Internet intensively to get information about products and manufacturers, and explore alternative distribution channels. Brand disaffection and betrayal appear as a major threat for institutionalized marketing and distribution arenas and can be interpreted as weak signals that announce a massive change in the values associated with consumerism in general (Marion, 2004).

In that perspective, the field of children's consumerism is quite interesting, as the tensions it undergoes can be considered as signs that herald a forthcoming major change in consumption practices. Slowly, parents are learning to reconsider their consumption habits in order to search for meaning and long-term social value in the selected products. Inventing a meaningful consumption will henceforth be the major challenge both for parents and industrialists aiming at children. This will lead to a dialectical confrontation of values, for instance in the ways described below:

Hedonist and pleasure	← vs →	Educational added value
Individual benefits	← vs →	Contribution to collective progress
Socially unacceptable	← vs →	Socially responsible
Short-term benefits	← vs →	Long-term systemic effects
Short-term employment	← vs →	Public future spending

This perspective highlights the fact that the relationship between the child and the market is always mediated by different institutions, resulting in a complex intertwining of logics, interests and values. Children-oriented commercial activities appear to constitute a highly ambiguous and controversial field upon which several institutions fiercely confront their ideological standpoints. On such a sensitive topic, forms of resistance to the ideology associated to mass consumption emerge with unusual intensity, thus ending in an attempt to reshape the field and define new criteria to assess the social added value brought in by firms.

The stake of responsibility: creating long-term social value:
The problem raised by the Globesity epidemic is a very clear illustration of the complexity of managerial action when aimed at children. The uncontrollable evolution of the epidemic is quite

---

[4] La distribution est désemparée face aux « alterconsommateurs », *Le Monde*, 15 July 2004.

frightening – USA, Canada, Great Britain and now France and other European countries - as it seriously endangers the global welfare system in all those countries. Not because of the series of illnesses provoked by obesity, but much more because of the necessity to fund huge investments in order to re-equip hospitals and clinics with suitably adapted furniture and therapeutic devices able to resist an average patient's weight increasing by 50%!

Of course, in all these cases, it is a quite dense group of causes that combine and contribute to creating, albeit several years after, an uncontrollable and unmanageable situation. Managerial action – marketing campaigns, etc. - is not the main cause, as there are demographic, sociological, cultural and political trends that favour the emergence of such phenomena. But it is quite obvious that managers cannot avoid reflecting on their own responsibility in the long term and the systemic consequences of managerial action aimed at children. Managerial practice is now pushed to take a more reflexive turn and to clearly state the way it conceives its long-term contribution to society. Firms eager for a long-term presence in children-oriented markets will need to make explicit their contribution in order to achieve more responsible marketing practices and to re-assess the actual meaning of mass consumption.

Achieving consistency in organizing industrial activities: Toy manufacturers and industrials in the clothing trade are in the front line when criticisms arise about the relocation of their industrial activities in search of a cheap labour force. Labelling products 'Child-free' or 'Ethique dans l'étiquette', or even organizing a surprise visit of their Asian subcontractors is not sufficient. SMOBY, the leading French toy manufacturer, has decided to solve that problem by directly buying subsidiaries in Thailand and China. The company has hired 12 engineers, who directly control the entire manufacturing process. As SMOBY runs its own factories, it can guarantee that no child is used in the production of their products. But the cost of this strategic choice is about 4% of the annual turnover, which is only partly compensated by the productivity and the low wages in that area.

Legitimizing the educational added value brought by its products or services: Educators and educational research have been part of LeapFrog's core assets since its foundation. As noted in the 2002 annual report, '*We believe that sound educational principles are at the core of the value of our brands or products*'. Its Educational Advisory Board, established in 2000, formally engaged the talents of leading educators towards creating mass-market learning products designed in accordance with established standards for age-appropriate learning. In addition to benefit derived from these nationally recognized experts, the firm benefited from the expertise of the many former teachers who had come to work at the company. In 2003, about one third of the total staff had been employed in the education sector at some point in their careers. Four educational principles:

- Children learn best when actively engaged
- Positive reinforcement and immediate feedback
- Ability-appropriate tasks motivate learners
- Supplemental materials should complement and enhance what children learn at school

Applegate and Dede, 2003.

The same kind of strategy is implemented by Bayard Presse, a leading French press group in the constitution of the editorial board of magazines aimed at children from 3 to 18 years old. This concern should lead industrials to accept having their products more systematically tested among parents and children by social scientists, such as psychologists or sociologists. Industrials will have to take part in some controversies about the most suitable educational principles to be applied to educative activities.

Choosing responsible marketing and promotional techniques: Until recently, the European Commission agreed that children constitute the most obvious group of 'vulnerable consumers' and were therefore entitled to particular protection. The 'Television Without Frontiers' Directive[5], which regulates television broadcasting and advertising, dedicates several articles on advertisements in relation to children, as well as specific provisions about the programmes children are likely to watch. The protection of children and other 'vulnerable consumers' stands high on regulators' agendas. The European Court of Justice (ECJ) stated repeatedly[6] that advertising ensures market access for products and increases consumer choice. The ECJ formulated the

---

[5]   Directive 97/36/EC of 30 June 1997 amending Directive 89/552/EEC on the
      Coordination of Certain Provisions laid down by Law, Regulation or
      Administrative Action in Member States Concerning the Pursuit
      of Television Broadcasting Activities, OJ L202/60 of 30 July 1997

[6]   Case C-412/93, *Société d'Importation Edouard Leclerc-Siplec* v *TF1 Publicité
      and M6 Publicité*, [1995], ECR I-0179 ; Joined Cases C-34/95, 35/95 and 36/95,
      Konsumentenombudsmannen v *De Agostini (Svenska) Förlag AB and TV Shop i
      Sverige AB*, [1997], ECR I-3843 ; Case C-405/98, *Konsumentenombudsmannen*
      v *Gourmet International Products Aktiebolag*, [2001], ECR I-1795.

concept of *'a reasonably circumspect consumer'*, able to adopt a critical attitude towards all sorts of promotions and offers. The aim is to ban commercial practices likely to materially distort the economic behaviour of a group of consumers that are particularly vulnerable to a product or practice because of their *'mental or physical infirmity, age or credulity.*

Committing far beyond self-regulating practices: In 2001, the European Software Association decided to launch a programme aimed at improving the information given about video games' content through the packaging. This positive initiative has to be related to the actual practices held by children when they buy video games. And what happens? Children buy games that do not suit their age: their video game library massively includes titles that are recommended for older children. This professional initiative was aimed at reassuring parents and preventing possible complaints, but as it turns out to be largely ineffective, can it be considered a truly responsible attitude?

The alternative solution of self-regulatory codes that replace laws in some countries and complement laws elsewhere will also be envisaged. Self-regulation is primarily a tool for advertisers, their agencies and the media to control the content of advertising which appears in business or consumer media. It is a system which enables advertisers to develop codes of practice in accordance with which they are prepared to act and by which they are prepared to be judged. The aim of self-regulation is to modify or moderate the content of advertising so that it complies first of all with the relevant European or national legislation and secondly with the prevailing national codes. Ideally, this activity should occur before the advertising appears. While this often happens, it is also certainly true that, in practice, there are times when advertising which contravenes either legal boundaries or self-imposed rules appears on TV or in other media.

Supporting educational initiatives about consumption: The current pressure on the food sector to respond to the political and media outcry on obesity is making food manufacturers look closely at their product ranges and at their marketing strategies. For example, a recent publication by Unilever, owner of some of the world's best known brands, says: *"Our vitality mission will focus our brands on meeting consumer needs arising from the biggest issues around the world today - ageing populations, urbanisation, changing diets and lifestyles.*[7]

---

[7] Dominic LYLE, Director General, EACA - Wednesday 14 July 2004 – UK Parliament.

In France, a new code on advertising to children developed by the industry is being amended by the Government after a debate in the Senate. Over and above the new industry code, the French Government has proposed that TV advertising messages for food products manufactured with the addition of sugar, fat, salt or synthetic sweeteners, broadcast from and received on French territory, must carry a specific health information message. Advertisers may derogate from this obligation provided they make a financial contribution to the National Institute for Prevention and Health Education. This contribution would be used to finance the production by the Government of nutritional information and education campaigns. All advertisers of food products whose nutritional composition may be harmful to children's or adolescents' health if consumed excessively will have the obligation of financing the production and broadcasting of a health information message on nutrition, to be aired within the same viewing time as the food advertisements.

Several other recent proposals were published by the Commission, including a Recommendation on the Protection of Minors[8], that suggest practical solutions such as media literacy programmes for minors and adults as a protection against potentially harmful programmes or websites. Companies operating on child-oriented markets would be inspired to proactively engage in such educational campaigns rather than waiting until enforcement measures are taken by governments.

Conclusion: Towards a transformational agenda for marketing management and research

Although children-oriented markets are constructed by some consultancy firms as a kind of Eldorado, our tentative reflections go clearly against such an interpretation and call for caution in managerial decision-making and practice when aimed at children.

From an academic standpoint, this analysis opens the way for a deep reappraisal both of marketing managers' responsibility in contemporary society and of the long-term contribution of marketing itself as a social institution.

---

[8] Recommendation of the European Parliament and of the Council on the protection of minors and human dignity and the right of reply in relation to the competitiveness of the European audiovisual and information service industry, COM(2004) 341 final, of 30 April 2004.

As consumers, citizens and researchers, we are still facing the deleterious effects of 'The Great Transformation' (Polanyi, 1944), which has led the economic realm to slowly drift away from political and social realms and to self-legitimize in a solipsist manner. As managers, researchers and citizens, can we accept that the economic circles develop on their own, regardless of social, political and ecological concerns? As researchers, we cannot escape the responsibility which is incumbent upon us to re-define the conditions under which we can develop more socially responsible research projects. This implies two major shifts: fostering an inter-disciplinary dialogue in research processes (Robertson and Feldman, 1976) and being willing to engage in the demanding discussion about the ethical preconceptions on which our theoretical frameworks are based.

It seems urgent to design a transformative agenda in marketing research in order to avoid reducing the child to a mere *'ego consumans'* (Baudrillard 1970: p. 121) and to promote socially responsible research practices and ethically embedded theoretical frameworks likely to contribute to a meaningful renovation of the finality of marketing discipline as a whole (Bergadaa, 2004).

References

Ansoff, I (1984); *Implanting Strategic Management*, Prentice Hall International.

Applegate, L.M. and C. Dede (2003); *Learning from LeapFrog: Creating Educational and Business Value.* Harvard Business School: Case Study, N° 9 – 804 – 062, November, 41 p.

Baudrillard, J. (1970); *La société de consommation – Ses mythes, ses structures.* Paris: Folio.

Bergadaa, M. (2004); Evolution de l'épistémè économique et sociale : proposition d'un cadre de morale, de déontologie, d'éthique et de responsabilité pour le marketer, *Recherche et Applications en Marketing, Vol.19, N°1*, pp. 55-72.:

Bourdieu, P. (1984); *Distinction – A social critique of the judgement of taste.* London: Routledge and Kegan Paul.

Brougere G. (2003); *Jouets et compagnie*. Paris: Editions Stock.

Bruner, J. (1990); *Acts of meaning*. Cambridge, Mass.: Harvard University Press.

Buckingham, D. (2000); *After the Death of Childhood*. London: Polity Press.

Certeau, (de) M. (1988); *The practice of everyday life*. Berkeley, CA: University of California Press.

Christensen, P. and A. James (2003); *Research with Children – Perspectives and Practices*. London: Routledge Falmer.

Cook, D.T. (Ed.) (2002) ; *Symbolic Childhood*. New York : Peter Lang.

Cross G. (2002); Valves of Desire: A Historian's Perspective on Parents, Children, and Marketing. *Journal of Consumer Research, Vol.29, December*, pp .441-447.

Dolto, F. (1985) ; *La cause des enfants*. Paris : Robert Laffont.

Douglas, M. (1996); *Thought styles – Critical essays on good taste*. London: Sage.

Gronow, J. and A. Warde (2001); *Ordinary Consumption*. London: Routledge.

IPSOS-Sofinco (2003); *L'influence des enfants sur le budget familial*. Etude européenne. *http://www.ipsos.fr/CanalIpsos/articles/*

Hite C. and R. HITE (1995); Reliance on Brand by Children, *Journal of the Market Research Society, 37:2,* pp.185-193.

Klein N. (2000); *No Logo*. Toronto: Alfred A. Knopf.

Kline, S. (2004), *Countering Children's Sedentary Lifestyles: An Evaluative Study of a Risk Media Education Approach*. Paper, colloquium Pluridisciplinary Perspectives on Child and Teen Consumption, Centre Européen des Produits de l'Enfant, IAE University of Poitiers, 25-26 Mars.

Kline, S. N. Dyer-Witheford and G. De Peuter (2003); *Digital Play – The Interaction of Technology, Culture and Marketing*. Montreal: McGill-Queen's University Press.

La Ville, (de) V.I. (2004) ; L'activité de consommation enfantine : les prémices d'un dialogue transdisciplinaire?, in N. Diasio (Ed.), *Au Palais de Dame Tartine - Regards Européens sur la Consommation Enfantine*. Paris : L'Harmattan, Coll. Dossiers Sciences Humaines et Sociales, pp. 27-41.

La Ville, (de) V.I. and V. Tartas (2005); L'activité de consommation enfantine et ses médiateurs, in V.I. (de) La Ville (Ed.), *L'enfant consommateur – Variations interdisciplinaires sur l'enfant et le marché*. Paris: Editions Vuibert (in print).

Le Bigot, J.-Y., C. Lott-Vernet and I. Porton-Deterne (2004); *Vive les 11-25 ans*. Paris, Editions d'Organisation, Eyrolles.

Maffesoli, M. (1996); *The time of the tribes – Decline of individualism in mass society*. London: Sage.

Marion G. (2004); *Idéologie marketing – Mal du siècle ?!*, Paris: Eyrolles.

Montandon, C. (1998); La sociologie de l'enfance: l'essor des travaux en langue anglaise. *Education et Sociétés*, *N°2*, Sociologie de l'Enfance, Tome 1, pp.91-118.

Ostergaard, P. and C. Jantzen (2000); Shifting perspectives in consumer research: from buyer behaviour to consumption studies, in S.C. Beckmann and R. Elliot (Eds.), *Interpretive Consumer Research – Paradigms, Methodologies and Applications*. Copenhagen: Copenhagen Business School Press.

Octobre S. (2004); *Les loisirs culturels des 6-14 ans*, Paris: La Documentation Française.

Page C. and N. Ridgway (2001); The impact of consumer environments on consumption patterns of children from disparate socioeconomic backgrounds. *Journal of Consumer Marketing, Vol. 18, Issue 1*, pp. 21-41.

Polanyi, K. (2003, 1944); *The Great Transformation*. Boston: Bacon Press.

Robertson T.S. and S. Feldman (1976); Children as Consumers: the need for multi-theoretical perspectives. *Advances in Consumer Research, Vol. 3, Issue 1*, pp. 508-512.

Russel R. and M. Tyler (2004); *The Handbags and the Gladrags: Gender and Tweenage Consumption*. Paper, colloquium Pluridisciplinary Perspectives on Child and Teen Consumption, Centre Européen des Produits de l'Enfant, IAE University of Poitiers, 25-26 Mars.

Siegel, D.L., T.J. Coffey and G. Livingstone (2002); *The great tween buying machine – Capturing your share of the multibillion dollar tween market*. Chicago: Dearborn Trade Publishing.

Singly, (de) F. (Ed.) (2004); *Enfants – Adultes : vers une égalité de statuts?*. Paris: Encyclopedia Universalis.

Singly, (de) F. (1996); *Le soi, le couple et la famille*. Paris, Nathan.

Sirota R. (1999); Les civilités de l'enfance contemporaine: l'anniversaire ou le déchiffrage d'une configuration, Dossier Sociologie de l'enfance 2, *Education et Sociétés, N°1*, pp. 31-54.

Tobin, J. (Ed.) (2004); *Pickachu's global adventure - The rise and fall of Pokémon*. London and Durham: Duke University Press.

Vygotski, L. (1933/1985); *Pensée et langage*. Paris: Editions Sociales.

8

Children as Change Agents in the Pursuit of the Competencies of the Future

ANNE FLEMMERT JENSEN

Prelude

For the past year, we have heard educators and business people express their serious concerns about the new generation of young people now entering the job market. They call them 'the curling generation'. Apparently, this is a generation who have grown up surrounded by concerned and caring adults who have swept away all obstacles for them in a misguided attempt at making life as convenient and carefree as possible. As a consequence, it is claimed that this is a generation who will tolerate no hardships. When they enter the job market, they expect the older generations to do the routine work, while they immediately dive into the new and interesting tasks.

This is not the first example - nor will it be the last – of adults who express their concerns about a generation. The stories are often different variations of the same two themes. In the case above, it was the story of 'the spoiled generation'. In other cases, we hear stories about 'the victimized generation'; for instance, when we hear the horrid stories about children whose development is crippled by the fact that they spend a large proportion of their everyday lives in front of a screen, being passively entertained.

Let me make one thing clear: It is always appropriate to be concerned about children's development and the potential ill-effects of new materials or objects offered to children. But the content of the debate is often misleading.

In the case of the so-called 'curling generation', the debate has taken a very critical turn. Several companies have announced publicly that from now on they will only hire people over 30 years of age. No one has made an attempt to put the debate into a more positive perspective. For the past 10 years at least, politicians, management gurus and industrial leaders have been propagating that the future work environment will be characterized by constant change and that we need to create a work force characterized by a higher degree of 'readiness for change'. 'Value driven leadership' has been another of the buzz words.

Now, apparently, we have a generation of young people who have grown up in a highly changeable society, where they have had the freedom, but also the responsibility, to find out what was right for them. They are not only used to constant change, but they actually thrive on it and expect it in their everyday work!! In many ways, they are the incarnations of what the management gurus and industrial leaders were crying out for. What a success! But instead we complain that they are spoiled and unfit for the job market, because they reject routine tasks and because their sense of loyalty is not to the same extent driven by external forces, such as a sense of duty or a fear of repercussions, but to a higher degree by internal forces, such as personal motivation and opportunities for continuous learning.

Background and purpose

Debates like the one mentioned above are often dominated by a view of children as cultural *becomings* who must be formed in the 'right way' and protected from the various negative influences of society.
The same is true when it comes to the ongoing debate about play, learning and creativity, which seems to be more relevant than ever. In 1999, LEGO sponsored the Next Generation Forum; a forum consisting of leading scientists from around the world who met on an ongoing basis to discuss how the present societal changes are affecting play and learning trends. They published an annual report called 'Toward the Creative Society', containing the main conclusions of their work. In the report, they claim that we are approaching a new kind of society called 'The Creative Society'; a society where play and creativity will be core competencies because they are going to be the seeds of future growth in the post-industrial world. This notion has been supported in various ways by researchers (Amabile, 1996;

Florida, 2002; Papert, 1993) as well as by politicians, industrial leaders and educators. And there is no doubt about it, the vast amount of research which is being conducted on an ongoing basis by LEGO Company shows that our values and attitudes towards play and learning are undergoing fundamental changes. Our research shows that this is affecting children's play practices and cultures as well as their learning styles. And it is putting new demands on educators and parents as well as companies targeting the children's market.

Like always, though, the debate has been dominated by concerned adults. A number of developmental psychologists (e.g. Elkind, 1988) are concerned about the fact that children increasingly engage in controlled and structured activities that have more to do with learning than with play. In this connection, the main fear is that children are not offered enough chances to develop skills like creativity, imagination and self-reflection; skills that are very important in a highly complex and diverse society. (Heffer, 2002), for instance, writes:

> 'A child who is constantly involved in all types of structured activities may not have the time to engage in important development activities such as self-reflection and self-evaluation.'

Some researchers point out that parents in contemporary western society tend to see and treat their children as status symbols. (Rosenfeld and Wise, 2001) refer to a term called 'hyper-parenting', writing that:

> 'The parents micro-manage every detail of their children's lives in what becomes a relentless pursuit of perfection. That drives kids to burn out before they even get their high school diplomas. [...]The kids are there to produce accomplishments. They're loved not for who they are but for what they can produce.'

Again, children seem to be victimized. But what if we try to view children as cultural *beings* whose attitudes, values and practices not only *reflect* but also *form* society. If we did that, we would often find that children's everyday practices are not only meaningful, when it comes to finding new ways of coping, new approaches to work or ways of utilizing new media and materials in creative ways, but their experimentation and exploration actually help create new structures and routines that may become guidelines for all of us in the future.

Why this interest from a toy company?

One might wonder why a toy producer like LEGO Company finds interest in issues like this. However, it has always been one of LEGO Company's distinct goals to offer children of all ages good play value and rich learning experiences. What is considered 'good play' and 'rich learning' today, however, is not the same as it was 10 years ago; in fact, the spheres of play and learning are undergoing a huge transformation, which is currently causing great turbulence on the toy market.

One of the changes that have taken place concerning the consumption of toys is the fact that mum and dad are no longer as central in the decision-making process as they used to be. Research conducted by LEGO Company shows that children start exerting an increasing influence on the decision-making process already from the age of three. By the age of five, parents are more or less reduced to gatekeepers.

This is supported by other research studies as well. According to (Deborah Roedder John, 1999), children today exert a considerable influence on purchasing decisions in families. A considerable number of research studies also show (e.g. Belch, Belch and Ceresino, 1985; Corfman, Harlam and Paschalina, 1996; Foxman Tansuhaj and Ekström, 1989; Lee and Beatty, 2002; Caruana and Vassallo, 2003) that children exert the greatest influence on purchases that are directly relevant to themselves, such as the purchase of toys, clothes and cereal products.

Children not only exert great influence on what their parents buy for them, but they also have more pocket money than ever before. According to (McNeal, 1999), children's spending power has exploded since the beginning of the 1990s. And according to, for example, (Hansen and Halling, 2002), a large proportion of the pocket money of Danish children is spent on toys and games, especially when it comes to the 5–12 year-olds, who are among LEGO Company's important target groups.

What is more, children today are brought up in a consumer society in which they are constantly bombarded with messages about brands and products. This means that they are extremely savvy consumers who know how to decode advertising messages and negotiate for the products and brands they want. They also know how to build their own identity and communicate it to others through the brands they surround themselves with.

Toys and other objects are meaning makers to children just as they are to adults. When children interact with objects and engage in play, they are performing very important rituals; rituals that allow them to make sense of themselves and the world. Children constantly explore and experiment with the boundaries of important dichotomies such as 'good and evil', 'right and wrong', 'girl and boy', and 'win or lose'. It also allows them to explore social concepts like 'the family' or 'motherhood'. But through their everyday practices, children do not just echo and reproduce existing attitudes, values and practices; they also create new ones that are better suited for the kind of everyday life they are growing up in and the kind of roles and tasks they are expected to fulfil.

In order to be attractive to children, toys and tools must help solve problems or offer opportunities and challenges. Toys and tools must allow children to tell stories about 'good and evil', 'girl and boy', and 'win and lose' that are coherent with today's values and attitudes. In all its complexity, it is really very simple: in order to be successful on the market today, toy companies need to have great insight into children's contemporary play cultures.

Results from LEGO Research among children

Over the years, LEGO Company has conducted considerable research among children aged 0-14. In the autumn of 2003, the LEGO Learning Institute commissioned an international anthropological study of children's play practices and ways of talking about their everyday lives. The research was headed by Professor Dominique Desjeux from the Sorbonne University in Paris, and comprised a team of sociologists and anthropologists.

The aim of the study was to gain insight into children's approaches to everyday life by observing and asking them about their play practices as well as their school and leisure time. This also involved asking them about their reflections concerning play, learning and creativity, as well as their representations of the future.

The study was conducted among children aged 8-14 in six different countries: Austria, China, France, Germany, Switzerland and the USA. The children were members of middle-class and upper-middle-class families. This naturally provides for a prejudice, which should be taken into account when reading the results.

The method used for the research study is called 'itinerary of objects'. The itinerary method comes from an anthropological practice, which has been adapted to fit to modern daily life. It entails following an 'object', such as a game or a play activity, through its use and its exchange, and the discussions or negotiations to obtain it, among some concrete actors. The aim is to understand how an object can be seen as a marker of passage between two stages or a belonging to one stage.

By analysing children's everyday practices in a wider socio-cultural context, we hoped to gain some insight into how children cope with the challenges and possibilities that face them in contemporary society.

Interviews

A total of 58 interviews were conducted with children. Each interview lasted from 1½ to 2 hours, and can be characterized as in-depth, semi-directive interviews with reconstruction of practice. They were conducted according to a written guideline composed of a set of semi-directive questions that the interviewers adapted according to the dynamics of the interviews.

Whenever possible, these interviews entailed the individuals actually using the object or carrying out the activity analysed in order to reconstruct their usual actions and procedures.

They also took the form of focused life-stories. The objective was to identify events in the life of the individual that are significant to the research questions, i.e. in the various stages of early childhood, childhood, pre-adolescence and adolescence.

These interviews took place on site, in the children's rooms or in their principal playing areas. The research team carried out the interviews in the native language of the children interviewed.

The children did not generally have trouble expressing themselves, even though a great number of follow-up questions had to be asked. In spite of initial shyness, the children generally became more talkative and quite enthusiastic as the interview progressed.

Photography

More than 1,000 photos were taken. The first level of use of these photos is illustration. However, the photos also represent a specific corpus of data that can enrich the research. The photos of the children's bedrooms are particularly interesting: firstly, for analysing the size of the children's rooms and the furnishing, layout and decoration of the child's space; secondly, for assessing the suitability of the room for play practices; and thirdly, for assessing the suitability of the various toys and play material for use in the children's room.

A written guideline defined specific themes in order to guarantee the gathering of similar photographs in all countries for comparison.

Parental authorization was obtained to allow for the scientific use, publication and exhibition of the pictures. The children themselves are not recognizably photographed. The pictures have been taken by the research team to guarantee a minimum quality.

Observation

This technique comes from ethnology and has been adapted to a western context. Observation can enrich the data collected throughout interviews. When opportunities arose, observations have been used. When appropriate, children were also put in specific play situations to help analyse their play practices.

It is important to emphasize that this study is not representative in any way. The specific aim was to gain deeper insight into children's life perspectives and representations; to move beyond the questions concerning *what* children prefer to do and *how* they like to spend time, and to seek deeper insight into *why* children have the preferences, attitudes and practices that they do. The most adequate methodology was a qualitative one, because it allowed us to ask the children directly about their practices and perceptions

The sort of general picture that children painted of society can be seen in Figure 8:1. Not surprisingly, it is a world that looks very much like the world we all inhabit: a media and technology driven world characterized by a great degree of individualism, fragmentation and diversity. Yet to children, that world looks distinctly different from the one that is often described by concerned adults. One of the main conclusions was that the children who were interviewed for this study did not seem to be marked by concerns. Rather, the focus seemed to be on the opportunities that this new world order offers to them; opportunities that arise from the freedom to choose what is right for themselves, and the possibility of entering into a never-ending learning process, of trying out different roles and identities, and of exchanging ideas and beliefs with others.

Figure 8:1.

The world according to kids

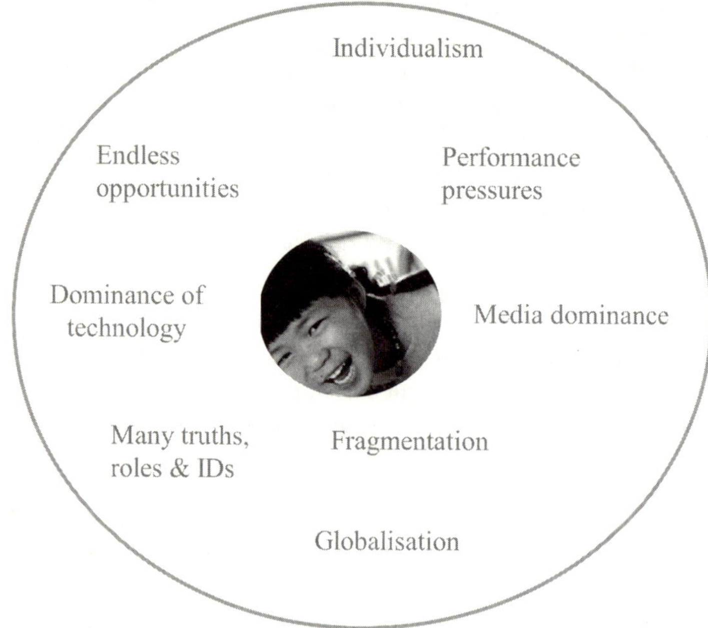

Source: A.F. Jensen, 'How children tell their future', 2004, unpublished.

Freedom, responsibility and performance

In the study, children paint the picture of a very individualistic society characterized by endless opportunities to reach personal and economic goals. They are aware that they have the freedom to choose whatever they want in life.

When they express doubts, they stress the difficulty of choosing. Raised in an environment that affords many opportunities, they wonder whether they will be able to set a goal for themselves and concentrate on achieving it. Aware that they must make choices to build their futures, children from 8 to 14 are involved in a search for their identity and their place in the world that sometimes causes them to worry about their ability to choose. Take, for instance, this very active 12-year-old Swiss girl, who says:

'I like to start things, but I stop a lot.'

The children in the study were very aware that freedom and responsibility are interlinked. They see it as a positive thing that they have the freedom to choose what is right for them, but they are also aware that the responsibility of turning into happy and competent people lies very much with themselves.

One of the most frequently mentioned fears among children in this study was the fear of failure; of not being able to live up to the responsibilities and expectations set by parents, school and society at large. This confirms the fact that children's innermost fears are formed by the fact that we live in a society characterized by increasing performance pressures.

At the same time, children display a distinct interest in not merely acquiring knowledge and information, but also in learning things in a meaningful and playful context and transforming this knowledge into enchanting stories and creative ideas. This is particularly evident when talking to children about how they would characterize the ideal school. The children have very vivid descriptions of what the school of their dreams is like.

At a time when some politicians in the Northern European countries, like Germany and Denmark, are talking about returning to more traditionalist forms of education such as learning by rote, restoring the authority of the teacher, etc., the children's thoughts about what makes up a rich learning environment goes in a completely different direction. The message from the children in this study was very clear: they want a school environment characterized by:

A high degree of autonomy, where they are actively involved in their own learning and where they have the possibility to choose between different subjects, come up with alternative solutions to problems, etc.

> '[I like music a lot] because we have a relatively nice teacher who communicates things quite well. He doesn't generally say, 'Now, you are going to do such and such', but 'Now, we're going to do that together'. It's more congenial (freundlich).'[1]

Learning how to learn - instead of learning how to do it. Children want to learn more than numbers and letters in a textbook. They want to conduct their own research, they want to learn how to write stories, and they want to learn how to apply existing knowledge to different situations. They want teaching methods that help them contextualize the learning.

---

[1] German boy, 13.

Learning through play. Children want to gain new knowledge through a playful approach characterized by exploration, exchanging of ideas, imagination, creativity and innovative thinking.

Learning by combining different media - written and visual, factual and more narrative, formal and informal.

> 'My German teacher, I think he knows a lot about history, and it is fun when he explains it. He isn't just talking all the time; he shows drawings and photos…In short, he makes all that clearer with a little irony, so we have fun (man Spaß hat). We don't just learn, we also have fun.'[2]

> '(A good teacher) counts like this:'3 candies plus 3 candies makes 6 candies.' That way you can really imagine it…A bad teacher will just say '3 plus 3 is 6'. He doesn't use such vivid examples.'[3]

Adapting to each child's needs. Children appreciate the right amount of difficulty. If the class work is too easy or if the children do not notice any personal progress, they lose interest. Learning has to match the needs of each student in terms of rhythm and variety of learning styles used.

> 'For example, geography is boring because you study what everybody knows about the earth; that it isn't flat, because she says that it is a disc. But everybody knows that this isn't true, and it is boring to repeat what we already did last year.'[4]

> 'I can't say that I read perfectly. I need a few more years to read as well as my grandmother. That is why I must really understand the English courses, because in the thick books, there are English words. But I have the impression that I'm learning less in school, because what I need is to learn by reading, not just to know how to read — that I know — but to know how to sort out information, to understand it.'[5]

Teachers acting as mentors rather than as authoritarian figures. Rather than forcing learning upon children, teachers must be open and broad-

---

[2] German girl, 14.
[3] Austrian boy, 9.
[4] German boy, 11.
[5] German boy, 10.

minded, and they must be able to listen and to adapt to children's different knowledge levels and learning styles. Moreover, they gain respect from being good at supporting children's own reflection and exploration process.

A spacious and enchanting physical environment that speaks to children's imagination and offers children challenges, mental well-being, a lot of space and the possibility of contact with people, nature and animals.

Postlude

One can say that children's approaches to learning and depictions of the ideal school provide a very precise analysis of what makes up a rich learning environment in our contemporary world. Our culture is characterized by a great degree of changeability, complexity, diversity and individualism. And to be able to navigate successfully in such a culture, it is simply not enough to recognize letters and numbers in a textbook, and act according to the instructions of a teacher - or a coming employer, if we refer back to the introductory example. In addition, one has to be able to apply existing knowledge to new situations, to tell intriguing stories, to find creative solutions to new and unexpected problems, and to choose among many different truths. As cultural beings who have never known another world, children have an intuitive understanding of what they need to learn and how they need to learn it. Instead of wanting to return to the sort of learning that was characteristic of our own childhood, or instead of complaining about the fact that children are too innovative and open towards change, we should start listening to them and learn from their approach to everyday life. Maybe we can gain important insight; firstly, insight into how to create a school attuned to the sort of learning necessary in the 21st century; secondly, insight into how to offer children of the 21st century toys and tools that they find intriguing and learn important things from; and lastly, and even more importantly, insight into how to build that future work force which will help Danish industry over the threshold and into the 21st century.

References

Amabile, T. M. (1996); *Creativity in Context*. Boulder, CO: Westview Press.

Belch, G. E., M. A. Belch and G. Ceresino (1985); Parental and Teenage Child Influences in Family Decision Making. *Journal of Business Research 13 (2)*, pp. 163-176.

Caruana, A. and R. Vassallo (2003); Children's perception of their influence over purchases: the role of parental communication patterns. *Journal of Consumer Marketing 20 (1)*, pp. 55-66.

Corfman, Kim, Bari Harlam and Paschalina (Lilia) Ziamou (1996); *Relative Influence of Parent and Child in the Purchase of Products for Children*. Presented at the Association for Consumer Research Conference, Tucson, AZ, October 1996.

Desjeux, Dominique and Sophie Alami (2003); *Play and Learning in a Changing World - Future perspectives provided by kids*. An international qualitative research project. Denmark: LEGO Learning Institute.

Elkind, D. (1988); *The Hurried Child: Growing Up Too Fast, Too Soon*. Massachusetts: Addison-Wesley Publishing.

Featherstone, M. (1991); *Consumer Culture and Postmodernism*. London: Sage.

Firat, F. and A. Venkatesh (1996); Postmodern Perspectives on Consumption, in R.W. Belk, N. Dholakia and A. Venkatesh (eds.), *Consumption and Marketing - Macro Dimensions*. Cincinnati: South-Western College Publishing, pp. 234-259.

Florida, R. (2002); *The Rise of the Creative Class*. Perseus Books.

Foxman, E.R., P.S. Tansuhaj and K.M. Ekström (1989); Adolescent's Influence in Family Purchase Decisions: A Socialization Perspective. *Journal of Business Research, vol. 17*.

Gabriel, Y. and T. Lang (1995); *The Unmanageable Consumer - Contemporary Consumption and its Fragmentations*. London: Sage.

Gray, J. (1999); *Men Are from Mars, Women Are from Venus, Children Are from Heaven*. London: Vermilion.

Hansen and Halling (2002); Økonomi og indkøbsindflydelse, in Hansen et. al., *Børns opvækst som forbrugere*. Copenhagen: Samfundslitteratur, pp. 235-258.

Heffer, R. (2002); *Overscheduled Kids May Miss Out on Important Benefits of Free Time.*
http://www.tamu.edu/univrel/aggiedaily/news/stories/01/022601-3.html.

Hill, M. (1997); *Hurry Up! It's Time to Go!* The Ohio State University, Co-operative Extension Service.

Jessen, C. (1999); *Det kompetente børnefællesskab - leg og læring omkring computeren*. Odense Universitet: Center for Kulturstudier.

John, Deborah Roedder (1999); Consumer Socialization of Children: A retrospective look at twenty-five years of research. *Journal of Consumer Research, April 1999*, pp. 200-201.

Lee, C. K. C. and S.E. Beatty (2002); Family structure and influence in family decision making. *Journal of Consumer Marketing 19 (1)*, pp. 24-41.

Longo, M. (1996); *Children and Stress: Are You Pushing Your Child Too Hard?* Home, Yard, and Garden Fact Sheet, 5152-96, Ohio State University Extension.

Manning, M. (1986); *Disappearing Childhood: 6 Going on 16*. Kappa Delta Pi Record, Fall, pp. 14-17.

McNeal, J. (1999); *Kids Market - Myths and Realities*. Paramount Market Publishing, Inc.

Papert, S. (1993); *The Children's Machine: Rethinking School in the Age of the Computer*. Harvester, Wheatsheaf.

Rose, M.A. (1991); *The Post-modern and Post-industrial: A Critical Analysis*. Cambridge: Cambridge University Press.

Rosenfeld, A. and N. Wise (2001); *The Overscheduled Child: Avoiding the Hyper-Parenting Trap?* N.Y.: St. Martin's Press.

Saxon, G. (1991); *Slowing Down Hurried Children*. Family Information Services, Minneapolis, MN.

Schor, E.L. (1995); *Caring for Your School-Age Child*. New York: Bantam Books.

Zimmerman, M. (1989); The Nervous System in the Context of Information Theory, in R.F. Schmidt and G. Thews (eds.), *Human Physiology*, 2nd ed., Berlin: Springer-Verlag.

Zlotnik, G. (2001); *De stakkels forældre*. Copenhagen: Reitzel.